W9-ACR-702

Birds of Texas

Field Guide

by Stan Tekiela

ADVENTURE PUBLICATIONS, INC.
CAMBRIDGE, MINNESOTA

To my wife Katherine and daughter Abigail with all my love

Acknowledgments

Special thanks to the National Wildlife Refuge System, which stewards the land that is critical to many bird species. Special thanks also to David Sarkozi for reviewing the range maps.

Edited by Sandy Livoti; Range maps produced by Anthony Hertzel
Book design and illustrations by Jonathan Norberg

Photo credits by photographer and page number:
Cover photo: Male Indigo Bunting by Stan Tekiela
Rick and Nora Bowers: 196 **Brian M. Collins**: 328 **Cornell Laboratory of Ornithology**: 108 (perching) **Dudley Edmondson**: 20, 26, 30 (soaring), 42, 102 (non-breeding adult, white juvenile), 110, 120 (female), 128 (female), 170 (both), 184, 220 (soaring), 222 (juvenile), 224 (Eastern perching and soaring), 242 (all), 274, 278 (male), 284 (male), 294 (perching, soaring), 300 (winter, displaying), 304 (soaring), 354 (juvenile), 358 (breeding), 378 (winter male), 382 (male), 390, 402 **Ned Harris**: 222 (perching, soaring, soaring juvenile), 248 (juvenile) **Kevin T. Karlson**: 24, 28 (soaring), 34 (male), 40 (male), 56, 58, 150, 190 (both), 356 (winter), 362 (winter) **Bill Marchel**: 4, 98 (male), 136 (white-striped), 166, 316 (both), 334 **Maslowski Productions**: 6 (male), 84, 90 (female), 116, 118 (Western), 134, 146, 156 (Eastern female), 232 (adult), 244, 250, 318 (male), 374 (chick-feeding adult), 394, 398, 404 **Steve Mortensen**: 44 (yellow-bellied male), 72 (both), 92 **Warren Nelson**: 44 (female), 108 (soaring), 172 (yellow-shafted female) **John Pennoyer**: 112 (female) **Johann Schumacher/CLO***: 98 (female) **Brian E. Small**: 28 (perching), 32 (Neotropic adult and juvenile), 36 (breeding and non-breeding males), 52 (female), 60, 70 (winter), 86 (both), 90 (male) 94, 118 (Eastern), 120 (Oregon female, pink-sided), 122, 124, 132, 138, 148 (winter), 156 (female), 172 (red-shafted male and female), 178, 182, 186 (breeding), 194 (male), 210, 214, 216 (male), 234 (both), 238 (perching), 254 (Oregon male), 264, 288, 318 (female), 322, 336, 338, 340, 342, 344 (yellow male), 348, 358 (winter, juvenile), 362 (breeding, in flight), 376 (male), 380 (female), 384, 392, 396, 400 (both), 406 **Stan Tekiela**: 2 (both), 6 (Eastern male), 8, 10, 12, 14, 16, 18, 22, 26 (in flight), 30 (perching), 32 (perching, drying wings, juvenile), 34 (female, juvenile), 38 (both), 40 (female), 46 (both), 48, 50 (both), 54, 62, 64, 66, 68 (both), 70 (breeding), 74, 76 (perching), 78 (both), 80 (all), 82, 88 (both), 96, 100, 102 (breeding, molting juvenile), 104, 106, 114, 126, 128 (male), 130, 136 (tan-striped), 140, 142 (both), 144, 148 (breeding), 152, 154, 158 (female, juvenile), 160 (all) 162, 164, 168, 172 (yellow-shafted male), 174, 176 (both), 180, 188 (all), 192 (both), 194 (female), 198 (both), 200, 202, 204, 206, 208, 212, 216 (female), 218, 226, 228, 230, 232 (cinnamon wing linings), 236, 240, 246, 248 (male, female), 252 (male), 254, 256 (all), 258, 260, 262 (both), 266, 268, 270, 272, 276, 278 (female), 280, 282 (both), 284 (female), 286 (perching), 290, 292, 294 (juvenile), 296, 298, 306, 308 (both), 310 (both), 312 (all), 314 (both), 320 (both), 324, 326, 330, 332, 344 (male), 346, 350 (male), 352, 354 (adult, in flight), 356 (breeding, both in flight), 358 (in flight), 360, 364 (both), 366 (both), 368 (all), 370 (both), 372, 374 (adult, in flight), 376 (female), 378 (male, female), 380 (male), 388 (both) **Brian K. Wheeler**: 76 (soaring, juvenile), 220 (Western perching and soaring), 238 (soaring, juvenile), 302 (both), 304 (soaring) **J. R. Woodward/CLO***: 286 (displaying) **Jim Zipp**: 52 (male), 382 (female), 386
*Cornell Laboratory of Ornithology

To the best of the publisher's knowledge, all photos were of live birds.

10 9 8 7 6 5 4
Copyright 2004 by Stan Tekiela
Published by Adventure Publications, Inc.
820 Cleveland St. S
Cambridge, MN 55008
1-800-678-7006
www.adventurepublications.net
All rights reserved
Printed in China
ISBN-13: 978-1-59193-045-7
ISBN-10: 1-59193-045-6

TABLE OF CONTENTS

Introduction

Sample Page

The Birds

Helpful Resources

Check List/Index by Species

About the Author

WHY WATCH BIRDS IN TEXAS?

Millions of people have discovered bird feeding. It's a simple and enjoyable way to bring the beauty of birds closer to your home. Watching birds at your feeder often leads to a lifetime pursuit of bird identification. The *Birds of Texas Field Guide* is for those who want to identify the common birds of Texas.

There are over 800 bird species in North America. In Texas alone there have been more than 500 different kinds of birds recorded throughout the years. These bird sightings were documented by hundreds of bird watchers and became a part of the official state record. From these valuable records, I've chosen 170 of the most common birds of Texas to include in this field guide.

Bird watching, or birding, is the most popular spectator sport in America. Its appeal in Texas is due, in part, to an unusually rich and abundant birdlife. Why are there so many birds? One of the reasons is open space. Texas is the second largest state, with over 267,200 square miles (694,700 sq. km) and about 21 million people. On average, that is only 79 people per square mile (30 per sq. km). Most live in and around four major cities in Texas.

Open space is not the only reason there is such an abundance of birds. It is also the diversity of habitat. Texas can be broken into four distinctive physiographic provinces or habitats–Coastal Plain, Central Lowland, Great Plains and the Basin and Range Province–each of which supports a different group of birds.

The Coastal Plain makes up most of eastern and southern Texas, a full one-third of the state. The region near the coast is flat and low-lying. There are 367 miles (591 km) of coastline along the Gulf of Mexico, with a total of 3,359 miles (5,408 km) of coast including the inlets and islands. The Coastal Plain is a great place to see hundreds of birds such as American White Pelicans and Caspian Terns.

The Central Lowland and Great Plains regions occupy much of central and northern Texas. This wide, expansive area with a few eroded river valleys is known for its large ranches and cattle grazing. It has a semiarid climate and is a great place to see the Roadrunner and Golden Eagle.

The Basin and Range Province lies to the west of the Great Plains in western Texas. This region has some of the finest scenery in the state and several mountain ranges, including Guadalupe Peak. Reaching an elevation of 8,749 feet (2,650 m) above sea level, it is the highest point in Texas. Here is a good place to see birds such as the Western Scrub-Jay.

Water also plays a big part in the bird populations of Texas. The Rio Grande Valley stretches along the Rio Grande River and makes up a 1,000-mile (1,610 km) border with Mexico. The Rio Grande carries little water during most of the year, but will flood after periods of heavy rain. This area is one of the best places in Texas to see birds. Its warm climate and water sources are great places for many wonderful birds such as the Green Jay and Plain Chachalaca.

Damming the rivers has resulted in forming most of the large lakes in Texas. The largest natural lake in the state is Caddo Lake, which is along the Louisiana border. It is not a single open body of water, but rather a winding network of channels. Several large artificial lakes include Lake Texoma on the Red River, Toledo Bend Reservoir on the Sabine River and Sam Rayburn Reservoir on a tributary of the Neches River. All of these lakes are good places to look for birds such as Blue-winged Teals and gulls.

Varying habitats in Texas also mean variations in the weather. Northern parts of Texas are cooler and moister than southern Texas. In fact, winters can be very cold in north central Texas. Southern Texas can be warm even during winter, and coastal Texas is very moderate by comparison. Western Texas can be very hot and dry during summer and cold in winter.

No matter if you're in the hot, arid deserts or in the cool, moist mountains of Texas, there are birds to watch in each season. Whether witnessing hawks migrating in autumn or welcoming back hummingbirds in spring, there is variety and excitement in birding as each season turns to the next.

OBSERVE WITH A STRATEGY; TIPS FOR IDENTIFYING BIRDS

Identifying birds isn't as difficult as you might think. By simply following a few basic strategies, you can increase your chances of successfully identifying most birds you see! One of the first and easiest things to do when you see a new bird is to note its color. (Also, since this book is organized by color, you will go right to that color section to find it.)

Next, note the size of the bird. A strategy to quickly estimate size is to select a small-, medium- and large-sized bird to use for reference. For example, most people are familiar with robins. A robin, measured from tip of the bill to tip of the tail, is 10 inches (25 cm) long. Using the robin as an example of a medium-sized bird, select two other birds, one smaller and one larger. Many people use a House Sparrow, about 6 inches (15 cm), and an American Crow, about 18 inches (45 cm). When you see a bird that you don't know, you can quickly ask yourself, "Is it smaller than a robin, but larger than a sparrow?" When you look in your field guide to help identify your bird, you'll know it's roughly between 6-10 inches (15-25 cm) long. This will help to narrow your choices.

Next, note the size, shape and color of the bill. Is it long, short, thick, thin, pointed, blunt, curved or straight? Seed-eating birds such as the Blue Grosbeak have bills that are thick and strong enough to crack even the toughest seeds. Birds that sip nectar such as Black-chinned Hummingbirds need long thin bills to reach deep into flowers. Hawks and owls tear their prey with very sharp, curving bills. Sometimes, just noting the bill shape can help you decide if the bird is a woodpecker, finch, grosbeak, blackbird or bird of prey.

Next, take a look around and note the habitat in which you see the bird. Is it wading in a saltwater marsh? Walking along a riverbank or on the beach? Soaring in the sky? Is it perched high in the trees or hopping along the forest floor? Because of their preferences in diet and habitat, you'll usually see robins hopping on the ground, but not often eating seeds at a feeder. Or you will see a Blue Grosbeak sitting on the branches of a tree, but not climbing down the tree trunk headfirst the way a nuthatch does.

Noticing what a bird is eating will give you another clue to help you identify that bird. Feeding is a big part of any bird's life. Fully one-third of all bird activity revolves around searching for and catching food, or actually eating. While birds don't always follow all the rules of what we think they eat, you can make some general assumptions. Northern Flickers, for instance, feed upon ants and other insects, so you wouldn't expect to see them visiting a backyard feeder. Some birds such as Barn Swallows and Cliff Swallows feed upon flying insects and spend hours swooping and diving to catch a meal.

Sometimes you can identify a bird by the way it perches. Body posture can help you differentiate between an American Crow and a Red-tailed Hawk. American Crows lean forward over their feet on a branch, while hawks perch in a vertical position. Look for this the next time you see a large unidentified bird in a tree.

Birds in flight are often difficult to identify, but noting the size and shape of the wing will help. A bird's wing size is in direct proportion to its body size, weight and type of flying. The shape of the wing determines if the bird flies fast and with precision, or slowly and less precisely. Birds such as House Finches, which flit around in thick tangles of branches, have short round wings. Birds that soar on warm updrafts of air, such as Turkey Vultures, have long broad wings. Barn Swallows have short pointed wings that slice through air, propelling their swift and accurate flight.

Some birds have unique flight patterns that aid in identification. American Goldfinches fly in a distinctive up-and-down pattern that makes it look as if they are riding a roller coaster.

While it's not easy to make these observations in the short time you often have to watch a "mystery bird," practicing these methods of identification will greatly expand your skills in birding. Also, seek the guidance of a more experienced birder who will help you improve your skills and answer questions on the spot.

BIRD BASICS

It's easier to identify birds and communicate about them if you know the names of the different parts of a bird. For instance, it's more effective to use the word "crest" to indicate the set of extra long feathers on top of a Northern Cardinal's head than to try to describe it.

The following illustration points out the basic parts of a bird. Because it is a composite of many birds, it shouldn't be confused with any actual bird.

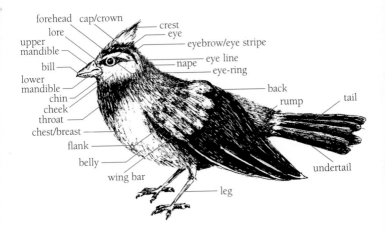

Bird Color Variables

No other animal has a color palette like a bird's. Brilliant blues, lemon yellows, showy reds and iridescent greens are commonplace within the bird world. In general, the male birds are more colorful than their female counterparts. This is probably to help the male attract a mate, essentially saying, "Hey, look at me!" It also calls attention to the male's overall health. The better the condition of his feathers, the better his food source and territory, and therefore the better his potential for a mate.

Female birds that don't look like their male counterparts (such species are called sexually dimorphic, meaning "two forms") are often a nondescript color, as seen with Indigo Buntings. These muted tones help hide the females during weeks of motionless incubation, and draw less attention to them when they are out feeding or taking a break from the rigors of raising their young.

In some species such as the Bald Eagle, Blue Jay and Downy Woodpecker, the male birds look nearly identical to the females. In the case of the woodpeckers, the sexes are only differentiated by a single red or sometimes yellow mark. Depending on the species, the mark may be on top of the head, face, nape of the neck or just behind the bill.

During the first year, juvenile birds often look like the mothers. Since brightly colored feathers are used mainly for attracting a mate, young non-breeding males don't have a need for colorful plumage. It is not until the first spring molt (or several years later, depending on the species) that young males obtain their breeding colors.

Both breeding and winter plumages are the result of molting. Molting is the process of dropping old worn feathers and replacing them with new ones. All birds molt, typically twice a year, with the spring molt usually occurring in late winter. During this time, most birds produce their breeding plumage (brighter colors for attracting mates), which lasts throughout the summer.

Winter plumage is the result of the late summer molt, which serves a couple of important functions. First, it adds feathers for warmth in the coming winter. Second, in some species it produces feathers that tend to be drab in color, which helps to camouflage the birds and hide them from predators. The winter plumage of the male American Goldfinch, for example, is an olive brown unlike its obvious canary yellow color in summer. Luckily for us, some birds such as the male Northern Cardinal retain their bright summer colors all year long.

Bird Nests

Bird nests are truly an amazing feat of engineering. Imagine building your home strong enough to weather a storm, large enough to hold your entire family, insulated enough to shelter them from cold and heat, and waterproof enough to keep out rain. Now, build it without any blueprints or directions, and without the use of your hands or feet! Birds do!

Before building a nest, an appropriate site must be selected. In some species such as House Wrens, the male picks out several potential sites and assembles several small twigs in each. This discourages other birds from using nearby nest cavities. These "extra" nests are occasionally called dummy nests. The female is then taken around and shown all the choices. She chooses her favorite and finishes constructing the nest. In some other species of birds–the Bullock's Oriole, for example–it is the female who chooses the site and builds the nest with the male offering only an occasional suggestion. Each species has its own nest-building routine, which is strictly followed.

Nesting material usually consists of natural elements found in the immediate area. Most nests consist of plant fibers (such as bark peeled from grapevines), sticks, mud, dried grass, feathers, fur, or soft fuzzy tufts from thistle. Some birds, including Black-chinned Hummingbirds, use spider webs to glue nest materials together. Nesting material is limited to what a bird can hold or carry. Because of this, a bird must make many trips afield to gather enough materials to complete its nest. Most nests take at least four days or more, and hundreds, if not thousands, of trips to build.

As you'll see in the following illustrations, birds build a wide variety of nest types.

ground nest **platform nest** **cup nest** **pendulous nest**

The simple **ground nest** is scraped out of the earth. A shallow depression that usually contains no nesting material, it is made by birds such as the Killdeer and Horned Lark.

Another kind of nest, the **platform nest**, represents a more complex type of nest building. Constructed of small twigs and branches, the platform nest is a simple arrangement of sticks which forms a platform and features a small depression to nestle the eggs.

Some platform nests, such as those of the Canada Goose, are constructed on the ground and are made with mud and grass. Platform nests can also be on cliffs, bridges, balconies or even in flowerpots. This kind of nest gives space to adventurous young-sters and functions as a landing platform for the parents. Many waterfowl construct platform nests on the ground, usually near water or actually in the water. These floating platform nests vary with the water level, thus preventing nests with eggs from being flooded. Platform nests, constructed by such birds as Mourning Doves and herons, are not anchored to the tree and may tumble from the branches during high winds and storms.

The **cup nest** is a modified platform nest, used by three-quarters of all songbirds. Constructed from the outside in, a supporting platform is constructed first. This platform is attached firmly to a tree, shrub, rock ledge or the ground. Next, the sides are constructed of grasses, small twigs, bark or leaves, which are woven together and often glued with mud for additional strength. The inner cup, lined with feathers, animal fur, soft plant material or animal hair, is constructed last. The mother bird uses her chest to cast the final contours of the inner nest.

The **pendulous nest** is an unusual nest, looking more like a sock hanging from a branch than a nest. Inaccessible to most predators, these nests are attached to the ends of the smallest branches of a tree, and often wave wildly in the breeze. Woven very tightly of plant fibers, they are strong and watertight, taking up to a week to build. More commonly used by tropical birds, this complicated nest type has also been mastered by orioles and kinglets. A small opening on the top or side allows the parents access to the grass-lined interior. (It must be one heck of a ride to be inside one of these nests during a windy spring thunderstorm!)

One of the most clever of all nest types is known as the **no nest** or daycare nest. Parasitic birds such as Brown-headed Cowbirds build no nests at all! The egg-laden female expertly searches out other birds' nests and sneaks in to lay one of her own eggs while the host mother is not looking, thereby leaving the host mother to raise an adopted youngster. The mother cowbird wastes no energy building a nest only to have it raided by a predator. By using several nests of other birds, she spreads out her progeny so at least one of her offspring will live to maturity.

Another type of nest, the **cavity nest**, is used by many birds, including woodpeckers and Western Bluebirds. The cavity nest is usually excavated in a tree branch or trunk and offers shelter from storms, sun, cold, wind and predators. A relatively small entrance hole in a tree leads to an inner chamber up to 10 inches (25 cm) below. Usually constructed by woodpeckers, the cavity nest is typically used only once by its builder, but subsequently can be used for many years by birds such as Wood Ducks, mergansers and bluebirds, which do not have the capability of excavating one for themselves. Kingfishers, on the other hand, excavate a tunnel up to 4 feet (1 m) long, which connects the entrance in a riverbank to the nest chamber. These cavity nests are often sparsely lined because they are already well insulated.

Some birds, including some swallows, take nest building one step further. They use a collection of small balls of mud to construct an adobe-style home. Constructed beneath the eaves of houses, under bridges or inside chimneys, some of these nests look like simple cup nests. Others are completely enclosed, with small tunnel-like openings that lead into a safe nesting chamber for the baby birds.

Who Builds the Nest?

In general, the female bird builds the nest. She gathers nesting materials and constructs a nest, with an occasional visit from her mate to check on the progress. In some species, both parents contribute equally to the construction of a nest. A male bird might forage for precisely the right sticks, grass or mud, but it's often the female that forms or puts together the nest. She uses her body to form the egg chamber. Rarely does the male build a nest by himself.

Fledging

Fledging is the interval between hatching and flight or leaving the nest. Some birds leave the nest within hours of hatching (precocial), but it might be weeks before they are able to fly. This is common with waterfowl and shorebirds. Until they start to fly, they are called fledglings. Birds that are still in the nest are called nestlings. Other baby birds are born naked and blind, and remain in the nest for several weeks (altricial).

Why Birds Migrate

Why do birds migrate? The short answer is simple–food. Birds migrate to areas with high concentrations of food, as it is easier to breed where food is than where it is not. A typical migrating bird–the Summer Tanager, for instance–will migrate from the tropics of Central and South America to nest in the forests of North America, taking advantage of billions of newly hatched insects to feed its young. This trip is called **complete migration**.

Some birds of prey return from their complete migration to northern regions that are overflowing with small rodents such as mice and voles that have continued to breed in winter.

Complete migrators have a set time and pattern of migration. Each year at nearly the same time, they take off and head for a specific wintering ground. Complete migrators may travel great distances, sometimes as much as 15,000 miles (24,150 km) or more in a year. But complete migration doesn't necessarily imply flying from the cold, frozen northland to a tropical destination. The Black-chinned Hummingbird, for example, is a complete migrator that flies from Texas to spend the winter in Central and South America. This is still called complete migration.

There are many interesting aspects to complete migrators. In the spring, males usually migrate several weeks before the females, arriving early to scope out possibilities for nesting sites and food sources, and to begin to defend territories. The females arrive several weeks later. In the autumn, in many species, the females and their young leave early, often up to four weeks before the adult males.

All migrators are not the same type. There are **partial migrators** such as Lesser Goldfinches that usually wait until food supplies dwindle before flying south. Unlike complete migrators, partial migrators move only far enough south, or sometimes east and west, to find abundant food. In some years it might be only a few hundred miles. In other years it might be nearly a thousand. This kind of migration, dependent on the weather and available food, is sometimes called **seasonal movement**.

Unlike the predictable ebbing and flowing behavior of complete migrators or partial migrators, **irruptive migrators** can move every third to fifth year or, in some cases, in consecutive years. These migrations are triggered when times are really tough and food is scarce. Red-breasted Nuthatches are a good example of irruptive migrators, because they leave their normal northern range in search of food or in response to overpopulation.

How Do Birds Migrate?

One of the many secrets of migration is fat. While we humans are fighting the battle of the bulge, birds intentionally gorge themselves to put on as much fat as possible while still being able to fly. Fat provides the greatest amount of energy per unit of weight, and in the same way that your car needs gas, birds are propelled by fat and stalled without it.

During long migratory flights, fat deposits are used up quickly, and birds need to stop to "refuel." This is when backyard bird feeding stations and undeveloped, natural spaces around our towns and cities are especially important. Some birds require up to 2-3 days of constant feeding to build their fat reserves before continuing their seasonal trip.

Some birds such as most eagles, hawks, ospreys, falcons and vultures migrate during the day. Larger birds can hold more body fat, go longer without eating and take longer to migrate. These birds glide along on rising columns of warm air, called thermals, which hold them aloft while they slowly make their way north or south. They generally rest at night and hunt early in the morning before the sun has a chance to warm up the land and create good soaring conditions. Birds migrating during the day use a combination of landforms, rivers, and the rising and setting sun to guide them in the right direction.

Most other birds migrate during the night. Studies show that some birds which migrate at night use the stars to navigate. Others use the setting sun, while still others such as doves use the earth's magnetic fields to guide them north or south. While flying at night might seem like a crazy idea, nocturnal migration is safer for several reasons. First, there are fewer nighttime predators for migrating birds. Second, traveling at night allows time during the day to find food in unfamiliar surroundings. Finally, nighttime wind patterns tend to be flat, or laminar. These flat winds don't have the turbulence associated with daytime winds and can actually help carry smaller birds by pushing them along.

HOW TO USE THIS GUIDE

To help you quickly and easily identify birds, this book is organized by color. Simply note the color of the bird and turn to that section. Refer to the first page for the color key. The Pileated Woodpecker, for example, is black and white with a red crest. Because the bird is mostly black and white, it will be found in the black and white section. Each color section is also arranged by size, generally with the smaller birds first. Sections may also incorporate the average size in a range, which, in some cases, reflects size differences between the male and female birds. Flip through the pages in that color section to find the bird. If you already know the name of the bird, check the index for the page number. In some species, the male and female are remarkably different in color. In others, the color of the breeding and winter plumages differs. These species have an inset photograph with a page reference and in most cases are found in two color sections.

In the description section you will find a variety of information about the bird. On page 1 is a sample of the information that is included in the book.

Range Maps

Range maps are included for each bird. Colored areas indicate where in Texas a particular bird is most likely to be found. The colors represent the presence of a species during a specific season, not the density or amount of birds in the area. Green is used for summer, blue for winter, red for year-round and yellow for areas where the bird is seen during migration. While every effort has been made to accurately depict these ranges, they are only general guidelines. Ranges actually change on an ongoing basis due to a variety of factors. Changes in weather, species abundance, landscape and vital resources such as the availability of food and water can affect local populations, migration and movements, causing birds to be found in areas that are atypical for the species.

Colored areas simply mean bird sightings for that species have been frequent in those areas and less frequent in the others. Please use the maps as intended—as general guides only.

Common Name
Scientific name

YEAR-ROUND
MIGRATION
SUMMER
WINTER

Size: measures head to tail, may include wingspan

Male: a brief description of the male bird, and may include breeding, winter or other plumages

Female: a brief description of the female bird, which is sometimes not the same as the male

Juvenile: a brief description of the juvenile bird, which often looks like the female

Nest: the kind of nest this bird builds to raise its young; who builds the nest; how many broods per year

Eggs: how many eggs you might expect to see in a nest; color and marking

Incubation: the average time parents spend incubating the eggs; who does the incubation

Fledging: the average time young spend in the nest after hatching but before they leave the nest; who does the most "childcare" and feeding

Migration: complete (consistent, seasonal), partial migrator (seasonal, destination varies), irruptive (unpredictable, depends on the food supply), non-migrator; additional comments

Food: what the bird eats most of the time (e.g., seeds, insects, fruit, nectar, small mammals, fish); if it typically comes to a bird feeding station

Compare: notes about other birds that look similar, and the pages on which they can be found

Stan's Notes: Interesting gee-whiz natural history information. This could be something to look or listen for, or something to help positively identify the bird. Also includes remarkable features.

winter

breeding

European Starling
Sturnus vulgaris

YEAR-ROUND

Size: 7½" (19 cm)

Male: Gray-to-black bird with white speckles in fall and winter. Shiny purple black during spring and summer. Long, pointed yellow bill in spring turns gray in fall. Short tail.

Female: same as male

Juvenile: similar to adult, gray brown in color with a streaked chest

Nest: cavity; male and female line cavity; 2 broods per year

Eggs: 4-6; bluish with brown markings

Incubation: 12-14 days; female and male incubate

Fledging: 18-20 days; female and male feed young

Migration: non-migrator

Food: insects, seeds, fruit; comes to seed and suet feeders

Compare: Similar to Common Grackle (pg. 13), but lacks its long tail. The male Brown-headed Cowbird (pg. 5) is the same size, but has a brown head and longer tail.

Stan's Notes: A great songster, this bird can also mimic sounds. Often displaces woodpeckers, chickadees and other cavity-nesting birds. Can be very aggressive and destroy eggs or young of other birds. The bill changes color with the seasons: yellow in spring and gray in autumn. Jaws are designed to be the most powerful when opening, as they pry open crevices to locate hidden insects. Gathers in the hundreds in autumn. Not a native bird, it was introduced to New York City in 1890-91 from Europe.

female pg. 141

male

Brown-headed Cowbird
Molothrus ater

YEAR-ROUND

Size: 7½" (19 cm)

Male: A glossy black bird, reminiscent of a Red-winged Blackbird. Chocolate brown head with a pointed, sharp gray bill.

Female: dull brown bird with bill similar to male

Juvenile: similar to female, only dull gray color and a streaked chest

Nest: no nest; lays eggs in nests of other birds

Eggs: 5-7; white with brown markings

Incubation: 10-13 days; host bird incubates eggs

Fledging: 10-11 days; host birds feed young

Migration: non-migrator in Texas

Food: insects, seeds; will come to seed feeders

Compare: The male Red-winged Blackbird (pg. 9) is slightly larger with red and yellow patches on upper wings. Common Grackle (pg. 13) has a long tail and lacks the brown head. European Starling (pg. 3) has a shorter tail.

Stan's Notes: A member of the blackbird family. Of approximately 750 species of parasitic birds worldwide, this is the only parasitic bird in the state, laying eggs in host birds' nests, leaving others to raise its young. Cowbirds are known to have laid eggs in nests of over 200 species of birds. Some birds reject cowbird eggs, but most incubate them and raise the young, even to the exclusion of their own. Look for warblers and other birds feeding young birds twice their own size. At one time cowbirds followed bison to feed on insects attracted to the animals.

female pg. 157

male

Eastern male

YEAR-ROUND
WINTER

Spotted Towhee
Pipilo maculatus

Size: 8½" (22 cm)

Male: A mostly black bird with dirty red-brown sides and white belly. Multiple white spots on wings and sides. Long black tail with a white tip. Rich red eyes.

Female: very similar to male, with a brown head

Juvenile: brown with a heavily streaked chest

Nest: cup; female builds; 1-2 broods per year

Eggs: 3-5; white with brown markings

Incubation: 12-14 days; female and male incubate

Fledging: 10-12 days; female and male feed young

Migration: partial migrator to non-migrator

Food: seeds, fruit, insects

Compare: Closely related to the Green-tailed Towhee (pg. 323), which lacks the bold black and red colors. Smaller than American Robin (pg. 285).

Stan's Notes: The Spotted Towhee and Eastern Towhee were once considered a single species called Rufous-sided Towhee. Found in a variety of habitats, from thick brush and chaparral to suburban backyards. Usually heard noisily scratching through dead leaves on the ground for food. Over 70 percent of its diet is plant material. Eats more insects during spring and summer. Well known to retreat from danger by walking away rather than taking to flight. Nest is nearly always on the ground under bushes, but away from where the male perches to sing. Begins breeding in April. Lays eggs in May. After the breeding season, moves to higher elevations. Song and plumage vary geographically and aren't well studied or understood.

female pg. 155

male

YEAR-ROUND

Red-winged Blackbird
Agelaius phoeniceus

Size: 8½" (22 cm)

Male: Jet black bird with red and yellow shoulder patches on upper wings. Pointed black bill.

Female: heavily streaked brown bird with a pointed brown bill and white eyebrows

Juvenile: same as female

Nest: cup; female builds; 2-3 broods per year

Eggs: 3-4; bluish green with brown markings

Incubation: 10-12 days; female incubates

Fledging: 11-14 days; female and male feed young

Migration: non-migrator to partial migrator

Food: seeds, insects; will come to seed feeders

Compare: Slightly larger than the male Brown-headed Cowbird (pg. 5), but is less iridescent and lacks Cowbird's brown head. Differs from all blackbirds due to the red and yellow patches on its wings (epaulets).

Stan's Notes: One of the most widespread and numerous birds in the state. It is a sure sign of spring when the Red-winged Blackbirds return to the marshes. Flocks of up to 100,000 birds have been reported. Males return before the females and defend territories by singing from tops of surrounding vegetation. Males repeat call from the tops of cattails while showing off their red and yellow wing bars (epaulets). Females choose mate and usually will nest over shallow water in thick stands of cattails. Red-wingeds feed mostly on seeds in fall and spring, switching to insects during summer.

female
pg. 165

male

Yellow-headed Blackbird
Xanthocephalus xanthocephalus

MIGRATION
WINTER

Size: 9-11" (22.5-28 cm)

Male: Large black bird with a lemon yellow head, chest and nape of neck. Black mask and a gray bill. White wing patches.

Female: similar to male, only slightly smaller with a brown body, dull yellow head and chest

Juvenile: similar to female

Nest: cup; female builds; 2 broods per year

Eggs: 3-5; greenish white with brown markings

Incubation: 11-13 days; female incubates

Fledging: 9-12 days; female feeds young

Migration: complete, to western parts of Texas, Mexico

Food: insects, seeds; will come to ground feeders

Compare: Larger than the male Red-winged Blackbird (pg. 9), which has red and yellow patches on its wings. Male Yellow-headed Blackbird is the only large black bird with a bright yellow head.

Stan's Notes: Usually heard before seen, Yellow-headed Blackbird has a low, hoarse, raspy or metallic call. Nests in deep water marshes unlike its cousin, the Red-winged Blackbird, which prefers shallow water. The male gives an impressive mating display, flying with head drooped and feet and tail pointing down while steadily beating its wings. The female incubates alone and feeds 3-5 young. Young keep low and out of sight for as many as three weeks before starting to fly. Migrates in flocks of up to 200 with other blackbirds. Flocks made up mainly of males return first in early April; females return later. Most colonies consist of 20-100 nests.

Common Grackle
Quiscalus quiscula

YEAR-ROUND

Size: 11-13" (28-33 cm)

Male: Large black bird with iridescent blue black head, purple brown body, long black tail, long thin bill and bright golden eyes.

Female: similar to male, only duller and smaller

Juvenile: similar to female

Nest: cup; female builds; 2 broods per year

Eggs: 4-5; greenish white with brown markings

Incubation: 13-14 days; female incubates

Fledging: 16-20 days; female and male feed young

Migration: non-migrator to partial in Texas; will move around to find food

Food: fruit, seeds, insects; comes to seed feeders

Compare: Male Great-tailed Grackle (pg. 21) is larger than the Common Grackle and has a much longer tail. The European Starling (pg. 3) is much smaller with a speckled appearance, and yellow bill during the breeding season. Male Red-winged Blackbird (pg. 9) has red and yellow wing markings.

Stan's Notes: Usually nests in small colonies of up to 75 pairs, but travels with other blackbirds in large flocks. Is known to feed in farmers' fields. Male holds tail in a vertical keel-like position during flight. The flight pattern is almost always level, as opposed to an undulating up-and-down movement. Unlike most birds, it has larger muscles for opening the mouth (rather than for closing it) and prying crevices apart to locate hidden insects. The name is derived from the Latin word *graculus*, meaning "to cough," for its loud raspy call.

Common Moorhen
Gallinula chloropus

YEAR-ROUND
SUMMER

Size: 14" (36 cm)

Male: Nearly black overall with yellow-tipped red bill. Red forehead. Thin line of white along sides. Yellowish green legs.

Female: same as male

Juvenile: same as adult, but brown with white throat and dirty yellow legs

Nest: ground; female and male build; 1-2 broods per year

Eggs: 2-10; brown with dark markings

Incubation: 19-22 days; female and male incubate

Fledging: 40-50 days; female and male feed young

Migration: partial migrator to non-migrator in Texas

Food: insects, snails, seeds

Compare: Similar size as the American Coot (pg. 17), which lacks the distinctive yellow-tipped bill and red forehead of Moorhen. Similar size as the Purple Gallinule (pg. 101), which has an iridescent blue and green body.

Stan's Notes: Also known as Mud Hen or Pond Chicken. A nearly all-black duck-like bird often seen in freshwater marshes and lakes. Walks on floating vegetation or swims while hunting for insects. Females known to lay eggs in other moorhen nests in addition to their own. Sometimes takes old nest in a low shrub. A cooperative breeder, having young of first brood help raise young of second. Young leave nest usually within a few hours after hatching, but stay with the family for a couple months. Young ride on backs of adults.

American Coot
Fulica americana

YEAR-ROUND

Size: 13-16" (33-40 cm)

Male: Slate gray to black all over. White bill with dark band near tip. Green legs and feet. A small white patch near the base of the tail. Prominent red eyes. Small red patch above bill between eyes.

Female: same as male

Juvenile: much paler than adult, with a gray bill and same white rump patch

Nest: cup; female and male build; 1 brood per year

Eggs: 9-12; pinkish buff with brown markings

Incubation: 21-25 days; female and male incubate

Fledging: 49-52 days; female and male feed young

Migration: non-migrator in Texas

Food: insects, aquatic plants

Compare: Smaller than most waterfowl. This is the only black water bird or duck-like bird that has a white bill.

Stan's Notes: An excellent diver and swimmer, often seen in large flocks on open water. Not a duck, as it doesn't have webbed feet, but instead has large lobed toes. When taking off, scrambles across surface of water with wings flapping. Bobs head while swimming. Floating nests are anchored to vegetation. Huge flocks of up to 1,000 birds gather for migration and during winter. The unusual common name "Coot" is of unknown origin, but in Middle English, *coote* was used to describe various waterfowl–perhaps it stuck. Like the Common Moorhen, American Coot is also called Mud Hen.

female pg. 183

male

Boat-tailed Grackle
Quiscalus major

YEAR-ROUND

Size: 16" (40 cm), male
14" (36 cm), female

Male: Iridescent blue-black bird with a very long keel-shaped tail. Bright yellow eyes.

Female: brown version of male, lacks iridescence

Juvenile: similar to female

Nest: cup; female builds; 2 broods per year

Eggs: 2-4; pale greenish blue, brown markings

Incubation: 13-15 days; female incubates

Fledging: 12-15 days; female feeds young

Migration: non-migrator; moves around to find food

Food: insects, berries, seeds, fish; visits feeders

Compare: Similar to male Common Grackle (pg. 13), but the male Boat-tailed has a distinctive long tail. Similar size as male Great-tailed Grackle (pg. 21), which is more common and widespread. Use geographical information to help identify. Look for an iridescent blue head and a very long tail.

Stan's Notes: A noisy bird of coastal saltwater and inland marshes, giving several harsh, high-pitched calls and several squeaks. Eats a wide variety of foods from grains to fish. Sometimes seen picking insects off the backs of cattle. Will also visit bird feeders. Makes a cup nest with mud or cow dung and grass. Nests in small colonies. Most nesting occurs in April and May. Boat-taileds on the Gulf coast have dark eyes, while Atlantic coast birds have bright yellow eyes.

female pg. 185

male

YEAR-ROUND

Great-tailed Grackle
Quiscalus mexicanus

Size: 18" (45 cm), male
15" (38 cm), female

Male: A large all-black bird with iridescent purple sheen on the head and back. Exceptionally long tail. Bright yellow eyes.

Female: much smaller than the male, brown overall, a gray-to-brown belly, light brown-to-white eyes, eyebrows, throat and upper chest

Juvenile: similar to female

Nest: cup; female builds; 1-2 broods per year

Eggs: 3-5; greenish blue with brown markings

Incubation: 12-14 days; female incubates

Fledging: 21-23 days; female feeds young

Migration: non-migrator to partial in Texas; will move around to find food

Food: insects, fruit, seeds; comes to seed feeders

Compare: Common Grackle (pg. 13) is smaller, with a much shorter tail. Male Brown-headed Cowbird (pg. 5) lacks the long tail and has a brown head. The male Boat-tailed Grackle (pg. 19) is found along the coast.

Stan's Notes: Our largest grackle, once considered a subspecies of the Boat-tailed Grackle. Prefers to nest near water in open habitats. A colony nester, males don't help build the nests, incubate or raise young. Males rarely fight, but females will squabble over nest sites and materials. Several females mate with one male. It is expanding northward, moving into northern states. Western populations tend to be larger than eastern. Song varies among populations.

21

American Crow
Corvus brachyrhynchos

YEAR-ROUND

Size: 18" (45 cm)

Male: All-black bird with black bill, legs and feet. Can have a purple sheen in direct sunlight.

Female: same as male

Juvenile: same as adult

Nest: platform; female builds; 1 brood per year

Eggs: 4-6; bluish to olive green, brown markings

Incubation: 18 days; female incubates

Fledging: 28-35 days; female and male feed young

Migration: non-migrator to partial migrator

Food: fruit, insects, mammals, fish, carrion; will come to seed and suet feeders

Compare: Similar to Chihuahuan Raven (pg. 25) and Common Raven (pg. 27), but has a smaller bill and lacks shaggy throat feathers. Crow's call is higher compared with Ravens' raspy, low calls. Crow has a squared tail. Ravens have wedge-shaped tails, apparent in flight.

Stan's Notes: This is one of the most recognizable birds in Texas. More common than its cousin, the raven. Often reuses nest every year if not taken over by a Great Horned Owl. Collects and stores bright, shiny objects in nest. Able to mimic other birds and human voices. It is one of the smartest of all birds and very social, often entertaining itself by provoking chases with other birds. Feeds on road kill but is rarely hit by cars. Can live up to 20 years. Unmated birds, known as helpers, help raise young. Large extended families roost together at night, dispersing during the day to hunt.

Chihuahuan Raven
Corvus cryptoleucus

YEAR-ROUND

Size: 20" (50 cm)

Male: A large all-black bird with a large black bill. Long bristle-like feathers cover more than half the length of the bill. Slightly shaggy throat feathers. Black legs and feet.

Female: same as male

Juvenile: similar to adult, but color of feathers on the neck is sometimes lighter

Nest: cup; female builds; 1 brood per year

Eggs: 5-7; gray to green with brown markings

Incubation: 19-21 days; female and male incubate

Fledging: 28-30 days; female and male feed young

Migration: partial migrator to non-migrator, to Mexico

Food: seeds, leaves, insects, fruit, small mammals

Compare: Common Raven (pg. 27) is very similar, but larger and has a lower-pitched call. The American Crow (pg. 23) lacks the shaggy throat and has a similar call, but it is lower in pitch than the Chihuahuan's.

Stan's Notes: Often confused with crows and other ravens. Usually found in open flat regions. Known to cache food. Male performs an impressive aerial display, soaring and tumbling, then standing in front of female with neck feathers fluffed. Builds a loose cup nest of sticks and lines it with hair and dry grass. Nest is usually solitary in a tree. Will reuse its nest several years in a row. Often breeds late in the season, presumably to time hatching with the flush of insects after the rainy season. Forms large flocks of up to several hundred after young leave the nest and throughout the winter.

in flight

Common Raven
Corvus corax

YEAR-ROUND

Size: 22-27" (56-69 cm)

Male: Large all-black bird with a large black bill, a shaggy beard of feathers on the chin and throat, and a large wedge-shaped tail, seen in flight.

Female: same as male

Juvenile: same as adult

Nest: platform; female and male build; 1 brood per year

Eggs: 4-6; pale green with brown markings

Incubation: 18-21 days; female incubates

Fledging: 38-44 days; female and male feed young

Migration: non-migrator in Texas; will move around to find food

Food: insects, fruit, small animals, carrion

Compare: Very similar to but larger than Chihuahuan Raven (pg. 25). American Crow (pg. 23) is smaller and lacks the shaggy throat feathers. Low raspy call, compared with the higher-pitched call of the Chihuahuan Raven and Crow. Glides on flat outstretched wings, unlike the slight V-shaped pattern of Crow.

Stan's Notes: Considered by some to be the smartest of all birds. Known for its aerial acrobatics and long swooping dives. Scavenges with crows and gulls. Known to follow wolf packs around to pick up scraps and pick at bones of a kill. Complex courtship includes grabbing bills, preening each other and cooing. Most begin to breed at 3-4 years. Mates for life. Uses same nest site for many years.

soaring

Black Vulture
Coragyps atratus

YEAR-ROUND

Size: 25" (63 cm); up to 4¾-foot wingspan

Male: Black vulture with dark gray head and legs. Short tail. In flight, all black with light gray wing tips.

Female: same as male

Juvenile: similar to adult

Nest: no nest on a stump or on ground, or takes an abandoned nest; 1 brood per year

Eggs: 2; light green with dark markings

Incubation: 37-48 days; female and male incubate

Fledging: 80-90 days; female and male feed young

Migration: non-migrator

Food: dead animals, occasionally captures small live mammals

Compare: Slightly smaller than the Turkey Vulture (pg. 31), lacking Turkey Vulture's bright red head. Turkey Vulture has two-toned wings, a black leading edge and light gray trailing edge. Black Vulture has shorter gray-tipped wings and shorter tail than Turkey Vulture.

Stan's Notes: Also called Black Buzzard. A more gregarious bird than the Turkey Vulture. In flight, the Black Vulture holds its wings straight out to its sides unlike the Turkey Vulture, which holds its wings in a V pattern. More aggressive while feeding but less skilled at finding carrion, it is thought Black Vulture's sense of smell is less developed than Turkey Vulture's. Families stay together for up to a year. Often nests and roosts with other Black Vultures. If startled, especially at the nest, it regurgitates with power and accuracy.

soaring

Turkey Vulture
Cathartes aura

YEAR-ROUND SUMMER

Size: 26-32" (66-80 cm); up to 6-foot wingspan

Male: Large bird with obvious red head and legs. In flight, wings appear two-toned: black leading edge with gray on the trailing edge and tip. The tips of wings end in finger-like projections. Long squared tail. Ivory bill.

Female: same as male

Juvenile: similar to adult, with gray-to-blackish head and bill

Nest: no nest, or minimal nest on cliff or in cave; 1 brood per year

Eggs: 2; white with brown markings

Incubation: 38-41 days; female and male incubate

Fledging: 66-88 days; female and male feed young

Migration: non-migrator to partial migrator in Texas

Food: carrion; parents regurgitate for young

Compare: Black Vulture (pg. 29) has shorter wings and tail. Bald Eagle (pg. 81) is larger and lacks two-toned wings. Unlike the Black Vulture and Eagle, Turkey Vulture holds its wings in a slight V shape during flight.

Stan's Notes: The vulture's naked head is an adaptation to reduce risk of feather fouling (picking up diseases) from carcasses. Unlike hawks and eagles, it has weak feet more suited to walking than grasping. One of the few birds that has a developed sense of smell. Mostly mute, making only grunts and groans. Seen in trees with wings outstretched to catch sun. Recent studies show this bird is closely related to storks, not birds of prey.

Neotropic
Cormorant

Neotropic
juvenile

juvenile

drying

Double-crested Cormorant

Phalacrocorax auritus

MIGRATION
WINTER

Size: 33" (84 cm)

Male: Large all-black water bird with long snake-like neck. A long yellow orange bill with a hooked tip.

Female: same as male

Juvenile: lighter brown with a grayish chest and neck

Nest: platform, in colony; male and female build; 1 brood per year

Eggs: 3-4; bluish white without markings

Incubation: 25-29 days; female and male incubate

Fledging: 37-42 days; male and female feed young

Migration: complete, to Texas, Mexico, Central America

Food: small fish, aquatic insects

Compare: Male Anhinga (pg. 35) has white spots and streaks and a long straight bill without a hooked tip. Similar size as Turkey Vulture (pg. 31), which also perches on branches with wings open to dry in sun, but Vulture has a naked red head. The Coot (pg. 17) lacks a long neck and long pointed bill.

Stan's Notes: Often seen flying in large V formation. Often roosts in large groups in trees near water. Catches fish by swimming with wings held at its sides. To dry off it strikes an erect pose with wings outstretched, facing the sun. The name refers to its nearly invisible crests. "Cormorant" comes from the Latin *corvus*, meaning "crow," and *L. marinus*, meaning "pertaining to the sea," literally, "Sea Crow." The Neotropic Cormorant (see inset) is found along the Gulf coast. It is smaller and thinner than Double-crested, and adult Neotropic has a white mark at base of bill. Map shows combined range.

female

juvenile

male

Anhinga
Anhinga anhinga

YEAR-ROUND
SUMMER

Size: 35" (88 cm); up to 3¾-foot wingspan

Male: All black with glossy green and white spots and streaks on shoulders and wings. Long neck and tail. Long, narrow yellow bill.

Female: similar to male, buff brown neck and breast

Juvenile: similar to female, light brown-to-white body

Nest: platform; female and male build; 1 brood per year

Eggs: 2-4; light blue without markings

Incubation: 26-29 days; female and male incubate

Fledging: 21-25 days; female and male feed young

Migration: complete to non-migrator, to coastal Texas and Mexico

Food: fish, aquatic insects, crustaceans and small mammals

Compare: The Double-crested Cormorant (pg. 33) is slightly smaller and lacks the white spots and streaks of male Anhinga. Cormorant has a shorter bill with a curved tip unlike the long straight bill of the Anhinga.

Stan's Notes: Also called Snakebird due to its habit of appearing like a snake–surfacing with just its head and long thin neck showing above the water. It skewers fish, a favorite prey, with its long sharp bill. Unlike ducks and other diving birds, its feathers become waterlogged, which helps diving and maneuvering underwater. Afterward, it often strikes a pose with wings spread to dry in the sun. A strong flier frequently seen soaring, it is confused with birds of prey. In flight, the long neck and tail help to identify.

female pg. 133

breeding male

non-breeding male

Lark Bunting
Calamospiza melanocorys

SUMMER
WINTER

Size: 6½" (16 cm)

Male: Short, stocky black bird with a large broad head, white wing patches and large bluish gray bill. Winter is black, brown, gray and white-striped with white wing patches.

Female: overall brown with a heavily streaked chest, white belly, black vertical line on each side of white chin, may have a dark central spot on the chest, faint white eyebrows

Juvenile: similar to adult of the same sex

Nest: cup; female builds; 1-2 broods per year

Eggs: 4-6; pale blue with markings

Incubation: 11-13 days; female and male incubate

Fledging: 8-12 days; female and male feed young

Migration: complete, to most of Texas, Mexico

Food: insects, seeds

Compare: The breeding male's bold black and white plumage is hard to confuse with any other bird's. Look for the rather large broad head and large bill to help identify.

Stan's Notes: Common in the dry plains and sagebrush regions of the state. Has short rounded wings. Flying with shallow wing beats, the male flashes white wing patches. Male takes to air to display to female, setting its wings in a V position and floating back, rocking like a butterfly, singing a most amazing song. Song is like the song of Old World larks, hence the common name. Will flock in fall with hundreds, if not thousands, of other Lark Buntings for migration.

male

female

Downy Woodpecker
Picoides pubescens

YEAR-ROUND

Size: 6½" (16 cm)

Male: A small woodpecker with an all-white belly, black-and-white spotted wings, a black line running through the eyes, a short black bill, a white stripe down the back and red mark on the back of the head. Several small black spots along the sides of white tail.

Female: same as male, but lacks a red mark on head

Juvenile: same as female, some have a red mark near the forehead

Nest: cavity; male and female excavate; 1 brood per year

Eggs: 3-5; white without markings

Incubation: 11-12 days; female and male incubate, the female during day, male at night

Fledging: 20-25 days; male and female feed young

Migration: non-migrator

Food: insects, seeds; visits seed and suet feeders

Compare: Almost identical to the Hairy Woodpecker (pg. 47), but smaller. Look for the shorter, thinner bill of Downy to differentiate them.

Stan's Notes: Abundant and widespread where trees are present. Stiff tail feathers help brace it like a tripod as it clings to a tree. Like all woodpeckers, it has a long barbed tongue to pull insects from tiny places. Male and female will drum on branches or hollow logs to announce territories, which are rarely larger than 5 acres (2 ha). Male performs most brooding. Will winter roost in cavity. Doesn't breed in high elevations, but often moves there in winter for food.

male

female

Ladder-backed Woodpecker
Picoides scalaris

YEAR-ROUND

Size: 7" (18 cm)

Male: Horizontal black-and-white zebra stripes on back, wings and tail. Red crown. Tan breast and belly with black spots. Black eye stripe. Black mustache mark. Dark bill.

Female: same as male, but lacks a red crown

Juvenile: similar to female

Nest: cavity; female and male excavate, then use wood chips to line hole; 1 brood per year

Eggs: 2-4; white without markings

Incubation: 13-15 days; female and male incubate

Fledging: 14-16 days; female and male feed young

Migration: non-migrator

Food: insects, fruit

Compare: Downy Woodpecker (pg. 39) and Hairy Woodpecker (pg. 47) lack zebra striping on the back.

Stan's Notes: Less common than other woodpeckers of arid desert scrub. Often probes for insects and larvae or feeds on cactus fruit. Male often feeds closer to ground than female; jumps to ground to grab an insect or pecks at the base of shrubs and trees. Female feeds higher up and probes less; pulls bugs from leaves or cracks in bark. A sharp "peek" call and short spurt of drumming. Will drum on a resonant log or tree to advertise territory ownership. Nests in dead branches of mesquite or saguaro cactus. Sometimes will excavate a cavity in a wooden post, yucca plant or utility pole. Common name comes from the black and white striping, resembling ladder rungs.

Black Phoebe
Sayornis nigricans

YEAR-ROUND

Size: 7" (18 cm)

Male: A black head, neck, breast and back with a white belly and undertail. Long narrow tail. Dark eyes, bill and legs. Can raise and lower its small crest.

Female: same as male

Juvenile: similar to adult, brown-to-tan wing bars

Nest: cup; female builds; 1-2 broods per year

Eggs: 3-6; white without markings

Incubation: 15-17 days; female incubates

Fledging: 14-21 days; female and male feed young

Migration: partial migrator to non-migrator; will move around after breeding to find food

Food: insects

Compare: Distinctive black and white pattern makes identification easy. Watch for tail to pump up and down very quickly when perched. Similar in size to Eastern Phoebe (pg. 267), which is gray.

Stan's Notes: Often seen in shrubby areas near water. Feeds mostly on insects near the surface of water. In the winter it feeds on insects near the ground. Like other flycatchers, perches on thin branches, flies out to snatch a passing insect and returns to perch. Pumps or bobs tail up and down quickly while perching. Male performs an aerial song and flight with a slow descent to attract a mate. Female builds shallow nest of mud, adhered to rocks or bridges, lined with hair and grass. Often uses same nest or location for several years.

male

female

Yellow-bellied Sapsucker
Sphyrapicus varius

WINTER

Size: 8-9" (20-22.5 cm)

Male: Medium-sized woodpecker with checkered back. Has a red forehead, crown and chin. Tan-to-yellow breast and belly. White wing patches flash while flying.

Female: similar to male, white chin

Juvenile: similar to female, dull brown and lacks any red marking

Nest: cavity; female and male excavate; 1 brood per year

Eggs: 5-6; white without markings

Incubation: 12-13 days; female and male incubate, the female during day, male at night

Fledging: 25-29 days; female and male feed young

Migration: complete migrator, to most parts of Texas, Mexico and Central America

Food: insects, tree sap; comes to suet feeders

Compare: The male Yellow-bellied Sapsucker shares the red chin of Red-headed Woodpecker (pg. 49), but lacks an all-red head. Female Yellow-bellied Sapsucker has a white chin.

Stan's Notes: Drills holes in a pattern of horizontal rows in small-to medium-sized trees to bleed tree sap. Many birds drink from sapsucker taps. Oozing sap also attracts insects, which sapsuckers eat. Sapsuckers will defend their sapping sites from the other birds. They don't suck sap; rather, they lap it with their long tongues. A quiet bird with few vocalizations, but will mew like a cat. Unlike other woodpeckers, drumming rhythm is irregular.

45

male

female

Hairy Woodpecker
Picoides villosus

YEAR-ROUND

Size: 9" (22.5 cm)

Male: Black-and-white woodpecker with a white belly, and black wings with rows of white spots. White stripe down back. Long black bill. Red mark on back of head.

Female: same as male, but lacks a red mark on head

Juvenile: grayer version of female

Nest: cavity; female and male excavate; 1 brood per year

Eggs: 3-6; white without markings

Incubation: 11-15 days; female and male incubate, the female during day, male at night

Fledging: 28-30 days; male and female feed young

Migration: non-migrator

Food: insects, nuts, seeds; comes to seed and suet feeders

Compare: Larger than the Downy (pg. 39) and has a longer bill. The Ladder-backed (pg. 41) has black-and-white zebra stripes on the back.

Stan's Notes: A common woodpecker of wooded backyards that announces its arrival with a sharp chirp before landing on feeders. This bird is responsible for eating many destructive forest insects. Has a barbed tongue, which helps it extract insects from trees. Tiny bristle-like feathers at the base of bill protect the nostrils from wood dust. Drums on hollow logs, branches or stovepipes in springtime to announce its territory. Often prefers to excavate nest cavities in live aspen trees. Has a larger, more oval-shaped cavity entrance than that of Downy Woodpecker.

Red-headed Woodpecker
Melanerpes erythrocephalus

YEAR-ROUND

Size: 9" (22.5 cm)

Male: All-red head and a solid black back. White rump, chest and belly. Large white patches on wings flash when in flight. A black tail. Gray legs and bill.

Female: same as male

Juvenile: gray brown with white chest, lacks any red

Nest: cavity; male builds with help from female; 1 brood per year

Eggs: 4-5; white without markings

Incubation: 12-13 days; female and male incubate

Fledging: 27-30 days; female and male feed young

Migration: partial migrator to non-migrator; will move to areas with an abundant supply of nuts

Food: insects, nuts, fruit; comes to seed and suet feeders

Compare: No other woodpecker in Texas has an all-red head. Pileated Woodpecker (pg. 73) is the only other woodpecker with a solid black back, but it has a partial red head.

Stan's Notes: One of the few woodpecker species in which male and female appear the same (look alike). Bill is not as well adapted for excavating holes as in other woodpeckers, so it chooses dead or rotten tree branches for nest. Later nesting than the closely related Red-bellied Woodpecker and will often take over its nesting cavity. Prefers more open or edge woodlands with many dead trees. Often seen perching on tops of dead snags. Stores acorns and other nuts. Nationwide populations are on the decrease.

male

female

Red-bellied Woodpecker
Melanerpes carolinus

YEAR-ROUND

Size: 9¼" (23 cm)

Male: "Zebra-backed" woodpecker with a white rump. Red crown extends down the nape of neck. Tan breast with a tinge of red on belly, which is often hard to see.

Female: same as male, but with a gray crown

Juvenile: gray version of adults, no red cap or nape

Nest: cavity; female and male excavate; 1 brood per year

Eggs: 4-5; white without markings

Incubation: 12-14 days; female and male incubate, the female during day, male at night

Fledging: 24-27 days; female and male feed young

Migration: non-migrator; moves around to find food

Food: insects, nuts, fruit; comes to seed and suet feeders

Compare: Similar to Northern Flicker (pg. 173) and Yellow-bellied Sapsucker (pg. 45). Note the tan chest and belly with obvious black-and-white stripes on the back. The Red-headed Woodpecker (pg. 49) has an all-red head.

Stan's Notes: Named for its easily overlooked rosy red belly patch. Mostly a bird of shady woodlands, it excavates holes in rotten wood looking for spiders, centipedes and beetles. Hammers acorns and berries into crevices of trees for winter food. Will return to same tree to excavate a new nest below that of the previous year. Often kicked out of nest hole by European Starlings. Gives a loud "querrr" call and a low "chug-chug-chug."

male

female

Golden-fronted Woodpecker

Melanerpes aurifrons

YEAR-ROUND

Size: 9½" (24 cm)

Male: Black and white zebra-patterned back with white rump. Black wing tips and tip of tail. Gray head, red crown and yellow-to-orange nape. Yellow patch at base of upper bill.

Female: same as male, but lacks the red crown

Juvenile: similar to female, but has a streaked breast and smaller yellow patch near upper bill

Nest: cavity; female and male excavate; 1-2 broods per year

Eggs: 4-7; white to cream without markings

Incubation: 12-14 days; female and male incubate, the female during day, male at night

Fledging: 28-30 days; female and male feed young

Migration: non-migrator; moves around to find food

Food: insects, nuts, seeds, berries; comes to seed and suet feeders

Compare: Similar to Red-bellied Woodpecker (pg. 51) in appearance and behavior, but male Red-bellied has a red nape. The Red-headed Woodpecker (pg. 49) lacks the black and white back and has an entirely red head.

Stan's Notes: Named for the yellow patch near bill. Often alone or in pairs. Prefers dry forests, cottonwoods near water and mesquite habitat. Works 6-10 days to excavate a cavity. Will use a nest box stuffed with sawdust. Male feeds female while she incubates. Less vocal than other woodpeckers. Caches food in crevices in bark. Hybridizes with Red-bellied Woodpeckers where ranges overlap.

Scissor-tailed Flycatcher
Tyrannus forficatus

SUMMER

Size: 10" (25 cm)

Male: White-to-gray head, neck, breast and back. Black wings with bright pink wing linings, seen in flight. Faint pink coloring on flanks and belly. An extremely long black tail with patches of white.

Female: similar to male, with a shorter tail

Juvenile: similar to adults, with a shorter tail, lacking pink underwings and sides

Nest: cup; female builds; 1 brood per year

Eggs: 3-5; white with brown and red markings

Incubation: 14-17 days; female incubates

Fledging: 14-16 days; female and male feed young

Migration: complete, to Central and South America

Food: insects

Compare: This flycatcher's extremely long tail and the distinctive black and white pattern with its pink wing linings make it hard to confuse with any other bird.

Stan's Notes: A wonderful summer resident. Like most flycatchers it hunts for insects by waiting on a post or low tree and flying out to capture them as they pass by. Drops to the ground to hunt for insects much more than the other flycatchers. Male performs an up-down and zigzag courtship flight, showing off his long flowing tail. Sometimes ends the flight with a reverse somersault. When not breeding, it often is seen in large flocks. Roosts communally, up to 200 individuals. Closely related to kingbirds.

winter pg. 293

breeding

Black-bellied Plover
Pluvialis squatarola

YEAR-ROUND
MIGRATION

Size: 11-12" (28-30 cm)

Male: Striking black and white breeding plumage. A black belly, breast, sides, face and neck. White cap, nape of neck and belly near tail. Black legs and bill.

Female: less black on belly and breast than male

Juvenile: grayer than adults, with much less black

Nest: ground; male and female construct; 1 brood per year

Eggs: 3-4; pinkish or greenish with black-brown markings

Incubation: 26-27 days; male and female incubate, the male during day, female at night

Fledging: 35-45 days; male feeds young, young learn quickly to feed themselves

Migration: complete to non-migrator, to coastal Texas, Mexico, Central and South America

Food: insects

Compare: Larger than the breeding Spotted Sandpiper (pg. 149), which lacks the black belly.

Stan's Notes: Males perform a "butterfly" courtship flight to attract females. Female leaves male and young about 12 days after the eggs hatch. Breeds at age 3. A common year-round resident along the coast. Begins arriving in July and August (fall migration) and leaves in April. During flight, in any plumage, displays a white rump and stripe on wings with black axillaries (armpits). Often darts across the ground to grab an insect and run.

Black-necked Stilt
Himantopus mexicanus

YEAR-ROUND
MIGRATION
SUMMER

Size: 14" (36 cm)

Male: Upper parts of the head, neck and back are black. Lower parts are white. Ridiculously long red-to-pink legs. Long black bill.

Female: similar to male, only browner on back

Juvenile: similar to female, brown instead of black

Nest: ground; female and male construct; 1 brood per year

Eggs: 3-5; off-white with dark markings

Incubation: 22-26 days; female and male incubate, the male during day, female at night

Fledging: 28-32 days; female and male feed young

Migration: complete to non-migrator in Texas

Food: aquatic insects

Compare: Outrageous length of the red-to-pink legs make this shorebird hard to confuse with any other.

Stan's Notes: Seen year-round along the coast and as far north as the Great Lakes. This is a very vocal bird of shallow freshwater and saltwater marshes, giving a "kek-kek-kek" call. Legs are up to 10 inches (25 cm) long and may be the longest legs in the bird world in proportion to the body. It nests solitarily or in small colonies in open areas. Known for transporting water with water-soaked belly feathers (belly-soaking) to cool eggs during hot weather. This bird aggressively defends its nest, eggs and young. Young leave the nest shortly after hatching.

female pg. 179

male

Bufflehead
Bucephala albeola

WINTER

Size: 13-15" (33-38 cm)

Male: A small duck with striking white sides and black back. Green purple head with a large white bonnet-like patch.

Female: brown version of male, with a brown head and white patch on cheek, just behind eyes

Juvenile: similar to female

Nest: cavity; female lines old woodpecker cavity; 1 brood per year

Eggs: 8-10; ivory to olive without markings

Incubation: 29-31 days; female incubates

Fledging: 50-55 days; female leads young to food

Migration: complete, to Texas, Mexico, Central America

Food: aquatic insects

Compare: Male Hooded Merganser (pg. 67) is similar, but lacks the male Bufflehead's white sides.

Stan's Notes: Common diving duck that travels with other ducks. Seen during migration and throughout winter, arriving in the state late in August. Found on rivers and lakes. Nests in old woodpecker cavities. Unlike other ducks, young stay in nests for up to two days before venturing out with their mothers. Female is very territorial and remains with the same mate for many years.

61

female pg. 201

male

Lesser Scaup
Aythya affinis

WINTER

Size: 16-17" (40-43 cm)

Male: Appears mostly black with bold white sides and gray back. Chest and head look nearly black, but head appears purple with green highlights in direct sun. Bright yellow eyes.

Female: overall brown with dull white patch at base of light gray bill, yellow eyes

Juvenile: same as female

Nest: ground; female builds; 1 brood per year

Eggs: 8-14; olive buff without markings

Incubation: 22-28 days; female incubates

Fledging: 45-50 days; female teaches young to feed

Migration: complete, to Texas, Mexico, Central America and northern South America

Food: aquatic plants and insects

Compare: The male Ring-necked Duck (pg. 65) has a bold white ring around its bill, a black back and lacks the bold white sides of the male Lesser Scaup. The male Blue-winged Teal (pg. 193) is slightly smaller and has a bright white crescent-shaped mark at base of bill.

Stan's Notes: A common diving duck. Often seen in large flocks on lakes, ponds and sewage lagoons. Completely submerges itself to feed on the bottom of lakes (unlike dabbling ducks, which only tip forward to reach the bottom). Note the bold white stripe under the wings when in flight. Has an interesting baby-sitting arrangement in which groups of young are tended by 1-3 adult females. A winter resident throughout Texas.

female pg. 203

male

Ring-necked Duck
Aythya collaris

WINTER

Size: 17" (43 cm)

Male: A striking duck with black head, chest and back. Sides are gray to nearly white. A light blue bill with a bold white ring and second ring at base of bill. Top of head is peaked.

Female: dark brown back, light brown sides, a gray face, dark brown crown, white line behind eyes, white ring around a light blue bill, top of head is peaked

Juvenile: similar to female

Nest: ground; female builds; 1 brood per year

Eggs: 8-10; olive gray to brown without markings

Incubation: 26-27 days; female incubates

Fledging: 49-56 days; female teaches young to feed

Migration: complete, to Texas, Mexico, Central America

Food: aquatic plants and insects

Compare: Similar size as male Lesser Scaup (pg. 63), which has a gray back unlike the black back of male Ring-necked Duck. Look for male Ring-necked's bold white ring around bill.

Stan's Notes: A common winter duck throughout Texas. A diving duck, watch for it to dive underwater to forage for food. Takes to flight by springing up off water. Was named "Ring-necked" because of the cinnamon collar (nearly impossible to see in the field). Also called Ring-billed Duck due to the white ring on its bill, and Blue Bill by duck hunters.

female pg. 205

male

WINTER

Hooded Merganser
Lophodytes cucullatus

Size: 16-19" (40-48 cm)

Male: A sleek black-and-white bird that has rusty brown sides. Crest "hood" raises to reveal a large white patch. Long, thin black bill.

Female: sleek brown and rust bird with a ragged rusty crest and long, thin brown bill

Juvenile: similar to female

Nest: cavity; female lines old woodpecker hole; 1 brood per year

Eggs: 10-12; white without markings

Incubation: 32-33 days; female incubates

Fledging: 71 days; female feeds young

Migration: complete, to the eastern half of Texas

Food: small fish, aquatic insects

Compare: A distinctive diving bird, look for the male's large white patch on the head and rusty brown sides. Male Bufflehead (pg. 61) is smaller than Hooded Merganser and has white sides. The male Wood Duck (pg. 327) is similar in size, but has a green head.

Stan's Notes: A small diving bird of shallow ponds, sloughs, lakes and rivers. Male Hooded Merganser can voluntarily raise and lower its crest to show off the large white head patch. Rarely found away from wooded areas, where it nests in natural cavities or nest boxes. Female will "dump" her eggs into other female Hooded Merganser nests, resulting in 20-25 eggs in some nests. Known to share a nest cavity with a Wood Duck, sitting side by side.

skimming

Black Skimmer
Rynchops niger

YEAR-ROUND

Size: 18" (45 cm); up to 3½-foot wingspan

Male: A striking black and white bird with black on top and white on bottom. Very distinct black-tipped red bill with lower bill longer than the upper. Red legs tuck up and out of sight when in flight.

Female: similar to male, only smaller

Juvenile: similar to adults, spotty brown on top

Nest: ground; female and male construct; 1 brood per year

Eggs: 3-5; bluish white with brown markings

Incubation: 21-23 days; female and male incubate

Fledging: 23-25 days; female and male feed young

Migration: non-migrator along coastal Texas

Food: small fish, shrimp

Compare: No other large black and white bird skims across the water like the Black Skimmer. In addition, no other bird has a lower bill that is longer than the upper bill.

Stan's Notes: Also called Scissorbill or Razorbill, referring to this bird's unusual, long bill. Uses its unique bill while in flight to cut through the water surface to catch fish or shrimp near the surface. Commonly feeds with several other skimmers. Often seen flying to and from nesting colony with fish in its bill. Nests in large colonies, often associated with tern species. Found along the Gulf coast.

winter

breeding

American Avocet
Recurvirostra americana

YEAR-ROUND
MIGRATION
SUMMER

Size: 18" (45 cm)

Male: Black and white back, white belly. A long, thin upturned bill and long gray legs. Head and neck rusty red during breeding, gray in the winter.

Female: similar to male, only with a more strongly upturned bill

Juvenile: similar to adults, with a slight wash of rusty red on neck and head

Nest: ground; female and male construct; 1 brood per year

Eggs: 3-5; light olive with brown markings

Incubation: 22-29 days; female and male incubate

Fledging: 28-35 days; female and male feed young

Migration: partial migrator to non-migrator in Texas

Food: insects, crustaceans, aquatic plants, fruit

Compare: White-faced Ibis (pg. 235) is larger and has a down-curved bill. Look for the rusty red head of breeding Avocet and upturned bill.

Stan's Notes: A handsome long-legged bird that prefers shallow alkaline, saline or brackish water, it is well adapted to arid western U.S. conditions. Uses its up-curved bill to sweep from side to side across mud bottoms in search of insects. Both the male and female have a brood patch to incubate eggs and brood their young. Nests in loose colonies of up to 20 pairs. All members of the colony will defend together against intruders.

male

female

Pileated Woodpecker
Dryocopus pileatus

YEAR-ROUND

Size: 19" (48 cm)

Male: Crow-sized woodpecker with a black back and bright red crest. Long gray bill with red mustache. White leading edge of the wings flashes brightly when flying.

Female: same as male, but has a black forehead and lacks red mustache

Juvenile: similar to adults, only duller and browner

Nest: cavity; male and female excavate; 1 brood per year

Eggs: 3-5; white without markings

Incubation: 15-18 days; female and male incubate, the female during day, male at night

Fledging: 26-28 days; female and male feed young

Migration: non-migrator

Food: insects; will come to suet feeders

Compare: Red-headed Woodpecker (pg. 49) is about half the size and has an all-red head, black back and white rump. Look for the bright red crest and exceptionally large size of the Pileated Woodpecker.

Stan's Notes: Our largest woodpecker. The common name comes from the Latin *pileatus*, which means "wearing a cap," referring to its crest. A relatively shy bird that prefers large tracts of woodland. Drums on hollow branches, chimneys, etc., to announce territory. Excavates oval holes up to several feet long in tree trunks, looking for insects to eat. Large chips of wood lay at bases of excavated trees. Favorite food is carpenter ants. Young are fed regurgitated insects.

Black-crowned Night-Heron

Nycticorax nycticorax

YEAR-ROUND
MIGRATION
SUMMER

Size: 22-27" (56-69 cm); up to 3½-ft. wingspan

Male: A stocky, hunched and inactive heron with black back and crown, white belly and gray wings. Long dark bill, short yellow legs and bright red eyes. Breeding adult has 2 long white plumes on crown.

Female: same as male

Juvenile: golden brown head and back with white spots, streaked breast, yellow orange eyes, brown bill

Nest: platform; female and male build; 1 brood per year

Eggs: 3-5; light blue without markings

Incubation: 24-26 days; female and male incubate

Fledging: 42-48 days; female and male feed young

Migration: non-migrator to partial migrator in Texas

Food: fish, aquatic insects

Compare: Yellow-crowned Night-Heron (pg. 309) has a similar size, a bold white cheek patch and lacks the black back of the Black-crowned. Half the size of Great Blue Heron (pg. 315) when perching. Look for a short-necked heron with a black back and crown.

Stan's Notes: A very secretive bird, this heron is most active near dawn and dusk (crepuscular). It hunts alone, but nests in small colonies. Roosts in trees during the day. Often squawks if disturbed from the daytime roost. Often seen being harassed by other herons during days.

soaring

juvenile

YEAR-ROUND

Crested Caracara
Caracara cheriway

Size: 22-25" (56-63 cm); up to 4-foot wingspan

Male: Black body and wings with a white chin, upper neck and wing tips. Large, obvious black crest. A long neck. Orange facial skin just behind a large gray bill. Long, strong yellow legs. White tail with a black terminal band, seen in flight.

Female: same as male, but slightly larger

Juvenile: similar to adult, but black areas are brown and white areas are tan

Nest: cup; female builds; 1 brood per year

Eggs: 2-3; white or pinkish with brown markings

Incubation: 26-30 days; female and male incubate

Fledging: 40-60 days; female and male feed young

Migration: non-migrator; moves around to find food

Food: carrion, small mammals, insects, reptiles

Compare: Osprey (pg. 79) is similar in size, but lacks the black belly and orange facial skin. Look for a bold black and white pattern and long yellow legs to help identify.

Stan's Notes: Largest member of the falcon family. Found in open savanna or desert scrub habitat, often near ranches. Feeds mainly on road kill, often coursing (patrolling) at low elevations on roads at sunrise. Very different from all other raptors in North America, using its legs to stalk and chase prey such as mice. Often seen with vultures, and often in pairs. Glides on flat wings unlike vultures in flight, which hold their wings upward in a semi-V shape. Roosts in trees at night. Facial skin can change color, usually to pale gray.

soaring

Osprey
Pandion haliaetus

MIGRATION
WINTER

Size: 24" (60 cm); up to 5½-foot wingspan

Male: Large eagle-like bird with a white chest and belly, and a nearly black back. White head with a black streak through the eyes. Large wings with black "wrist" marks. Dark bill.

Female: same as male, but larger with a necklace of brown streaking

Juvenile: similar to adults, with a light tan breast

Nest: platform, often on raised wooden platform; female and male build; 1 brood per year

Eggs: 2-4; white with brown markings

Incubation: 32-42 days; female and male incubate

Fledging: 48-58 days; male and female feed young

Migration: complete, to coastal Texas, Mexico, Central America and South America

Food: fish

Compare: Bald Eagle (pg. 81) is on average 10 inches (25 cm) larger with an all-white head and tail. The juvenile Bald Eagle is brown with white speckles. Look for a white belly and dark stripe through eyes to identify Osprey.

Stan's Notes: Ospreys are in a family all their own. It is the only raptor that plunges into water feet first to catch fish. Can hover for a few seconds before diving. Carries fish in a head-first position for better aerodynamics. Often harassed by Bald Eagles for its catch. In flight, wings are angled (cocked) backward. Nests on man-made towers and in tall dead trees. Recent studies show male and female might mate for life. May not migrate to same wintering grounds.

soaring

juvenile

soaring
juvenile

Bald Eagle
Haliaeetus leucocephalus

YEAR-ROUND
WINTER

Size: 31-37" (79-94 cm); up to 7-foot wingspan

Male: Pure white head and tail contrast with dark brown-to-black body and wings. A large, curved yellow bill and yellow feet.

Female: same as male, only slightly larger

Juvenile: dark brown with white spots or speckles throughout body and wings, gray bill

Nest: massive platform, usually in a tree; female and male build; 1 brood per year

Eggs: 2; off-white without markings

Incubation: 34-36 days; female and male incubate

Fledging: 75-90 days; female and male feed young

Migration: partial migrator to non-migrator in Texas

Food: fish, carrion, birds (mainly ducks)

Compare: The Golden Eagle (pg. 239), Black Vulture (pg. 29) and Turkey Vulture (pg. 31) lack the white head and white tail of adult Bald Eagle. The juvenile Golden Eagle, with its white wrist marks and white base of tail, is similar to the juvenile Bald Eagle.

Stan's Notes: Driven to near extinction due to DDT poisoning and illegal killing. Now making a comeback in North America. Returns to same nest each year, adding more sticks, enlarging it to massive proportions, at times up to 1,000 pounds (450 kg). In the midair mating ritual, one eagle will flip upside down and lock talons with another. Both tumble, then break apart to continue flight. Thought to mate for life, but will switch mates if not successful reproducing. Juvenile attains the white head and tail at about 4-5 years of age.

female pg. 123

male

Indigo Bunting
Passerina cyanea

MIGRATION
SUMMER

Size: 5½" (14 cm)

Male: Vibrant blue finch-like bird. Scattered dark markings on wings and tail.

Female: light brown bird with faint markings

Juvenile: similar to female

Nest: cup; female builds; 2 broods per year

Eggs: 3-4; pale blue without markings

Incubation: 12-13 days; female incubates

Fledging: 10-11 days; female feeds young

Migration: complete, to Mexico, Central America and South America

Food: insects, seeds, fruit; will visit seed feeders

Compare: The male Eastern and Western Bluebirds (pp. 89 and 91) are larger and have a rusty red breast. Male Mountain Bluebird (pg. 87) has a thin black bill and white lower belly.

Stan's Notes: Usually only the males are noticed. Actually a black bird, as it doesn't have any blue pigment in its feathers. As with the Blue Jay, sunlight is refracted within the structure of the bunting's feathers, making them appear blue. Appears iridescent in direct sun. Molts to acquire body feathers with gray tips, which quickly wear off to reveal bright blue plumage in spring. Molts in fall to appear like females during winter. Males often sing from treetops to attract mates. Will come to feeders in spring before insects are plentiful. Mostly seen along woodland edges, feeding on insects. Migrates at night in flocks of 5-10 birds. Males return before the females and juveniles, usually returning to previous year's nest site. Juveniles move to within a mile from birth site.

female
pg. 139

male

Blue Grosbeak
Passerina caerulea

MIGRATION
SUMMER

Size:	7" (18 cm)
Male:	Overall blue bird with 2 chestnut wing bars. Large gray-to-silver bill. Black around base of bill.
Female:	overall brown with darker wings and tail, 2 tan wing bars, large gray-to-silver bill
Juvenile:	similar to female
Nest:	cup; female builds; 1-2 broods per year
Eggs:	3-6; pale blue without markings
Incubation:	11-12 days; female incubates
Fledging:	9-10 days; female and male feed young
Migration:	complete, to Mexico and Central America
Food:	insects, seeds; will come to seed feeders
Compare:	The male Indigo Bunting (pg. 83) is smaller and lacks wing bars. Male Mountain and Western Bluebirds (pp. 87 and 89) are the same size, but lack chestnut wing bars and the oversized bill.

Stan's Notes: This grosbeak returns to Texas by early May. It has expanded northward with overall populations increasing over the past 30-40 years. A bird of semi-open habitats such as overgrown fields, riversides, woodland edges and fencerows. Frequently seen twitching and spreading its tail. First-year males show only some blue, obtaining the full complement of blue feathers in the second winter. Visits seed feeders.

male

female

Mountain Bluebird
Sialia currucoides

WINTER

Size: 7" (18 cm)

Male: An overall sky blue bird with a darker blue head, back, wings and tail and white lower belly. Thin black bill.

Female: similar to male, but paler with a nearly gray head and chest and a whitish belly

Juvenile: similar to adult of the same sex

Nest: cavity, old woodpecker cavity, wooden nest box; female builds; 1-2 broods per year

Eggs: 4-6; pale blue without markings

Incubation: 13-14 days; female incubates

Fledging: 22-23 days; female and male feed young

Migration: complete, to parts of Texas, Mexico

Food: insects

Compare: Similar to Eastern and Western Bluebirds (pp. 89 and 91), but lacks the rusty red chest. Same size as the male Blue Grosbeak (pg. 85), but lacks Grosbeak's chestnut wing bars and oversized bill. Male Indigo Bunting (pg. 83) is smaller and lacks the white lower belly.

Stan's Notes: This bird is common in open mountainous country. Due to conservation of suitable nest sites (dead trees with cavities and man-made nest boxes), populations increased over the past 30 years. Like other bluebirds, Mountain Bluebirds take well to nest boxes and tolerate close contact with humans. Young will imprint on their first nest box or cavity, then choose a similar type of box or cavity throughout the rest of life.

male

female

Eastern Bluebird
Sialia sialis

YEAR-ROUND
WINTER

Size: 7" (18 cm)

Male: Reminiscent of its larger cousin, American Robin, with a rusty red breast and a white belly. Sky blue head, back and tail.

Female: shares rusty red breast and white belly, but is grayer with faint blue tail and wings

Juvenile: similar to female, with spots on chest, blue wing markings

Nest: cavity, old woodpecker cavity or man-made nest box; female builds; 2 broods per year

Eggs: 4-5; pale blue without markings

Incubation: 12-14 days; female incubates

Fledging: 15-18 days; male and female feed young

Migration: complete to non-migrator in Texas

Food: insects, fruit

Compare: Male Western Bluebird (pg. 91) has a blue throat and is rusty red on flanks. Mountain Bluebird (pg. 87) and male Indigo Bunting (pg. 83) lack a rusty red chest. The Blue Jay (pg. 97) is much larger and has a crest.

Stan's Notes: Once nearly eliminated from Texas due to a lack of nest cavities, bluebirds have made a remarkable comeback with the aid of bird enthusiasts who have put up thousands of bluebird nest boxes. Easily tamed, will come to a shallow dish with mealworms. Bluebirds like open habitats such as fields, pastures and roadsides. Will perch in trees or on fence posts and wait for grasshoppers. Gives a distinctive "chur-lee chur chur-lee" song. Young of first brood help raise young of second.

Western Bluebird
Sialia mexicana

YEAR-ROUND
WINTER

Size: 7" (18 cm)

Male: Deep blue head, neck, throat, back, wings and tail. Rusty red chest and flanks.

Female: similar to male, only duller with gray head

Juvenile: similar to female, with a speckled chest

Nest: cavity, old woodpecker cavity, wooden nest box; female builds; 1-2 broods per year

Eggs: 4-6; pale blue without markings

Incubation: 13-14 days; female incubates

Fledging: 22-23 days; female and male feed young

Migration: non-migrator to partial migrator in Texas

Food: insects, fruit

Compare: The male Eastern Bluebird (pg. 89) looks very similar, but lacks male Western's blue throat and rusty red on flanks. Mountain Bluebird (pg. 87) and male Indigo Bunting (pg. 83) are similar, but lack the rusty red breast. Male Blue Grosbeak (pg. 85) is the same size, but has chestnut wing bars and an oversized bill.

Stan's Notes: Found in a variety of habitats, from agricultural land to clear-cuts. Requires a cavity for nesting. Competes with starlings for nest cavities. Like Mountain Bluebirds, it uses nest boxes, which are responsible for the stable populations. The courting male will fly in front of the female, spreading wings and tail, then perch next to her. Often seen going in and out of nest box or cavity as if to say, "Look inside." Male may offer food to female to establish pair bond.

Barn Swallow
Hirundo rustica

SUMMER

Size: 7" (18 cm)

Male: A sleek swallow with a blue black back, a cinnamon belly and reddish brown chin. White spots on long forked tail.

Female: same as male, only slightly duller

Juvenile: similar to adults, with a tan belly and chin, and shorter tail

Nest: cup; female and male construct; 2 broods per year

Eggs: 4-5; white with brown markings

Incubation: 13-17 days; female incubates

Fledging: 18-23 days; female and male feed young

Migration: complete, to South America

Food: insects, prefers beetles, wasps and flies

Compare: The Cliff Swallow (pg. 125) is smaller and lacks a distinctive, deeply forked tail. The Chimney Swift (pg. 109) has a narrow pointed tail and longer wings than body.

Stan's Notes: Of the seven swallow species in Texas, this is the only one with a deeply forked tail. Unlike other swallows, Barn Swallow rarely glides in flight, so look for continuous flapping. It builds a mud nest using up to 1,000 beak-loads of mud, often in or on barns. Nests in colonies of 4-6 individuals, but nesting alone isn't uncommon. Drinks in flight, skimming water or getting water from wet leaves. Also bathes while flying through rain or sprinklers.

Western Scrub-Jay
Aphelocoma californica

YEAR-ROUND

Size: 11" (28 cm)

Male: Blue head, wings, tail and breast band with a brownish patch on back. Dull white chin, breast and belly. Very long tail.

Female: same as male

Juvenile: similar to adult, overall gray with light blue wings and tail

Nest: cup; female and male construct; 1 brood per year

Eggs: 3-6; pale green with red brown markings

Incubation: 15-17 days; female incubates

Fledging: 18-20 days; female and male feed young

Migration: non-migrator

Food: insects, seeds, fruit; comes to seed feeders

Compare: Blue Jay (pg. 97) is similar in size, but has a black necklace and crest. Look for Western Scrub-Jay's brownish patch on the back and white chin to help identify.

Stan's Notes: A tame bird of urban areas that visits feeders. Several subspecies occur with some regional variations in color, the Interior race (shown) being a paler blue. Forms a long-term pair bond, with the male feeding female before and during incubation. Young of a pair remain close by for up to a couple years, helping parents raise subsequent brothers and sisters. Caches food by burying it for later consumption. Likely serves as a major distributor of oaks and pines by not returning to eat the seeds it buried.

Blue Jay
Cyanocitta cristata

YEAR-ROUND

Size: 12" (30 cm)

Male: Large, bright light blue and white bird with a black necklace. Crest moves up and down at will. White face with a gray belly. White wing bars on blue wings. Black spots and a white tip on blue tail.

Female: same as male

Juvenile: same as adult, only duller

Nest: cup; female and male construct; 1-2 broods per year

Eggs: 4-5; green to blue with brown markings

Incubation: 16-18 days; female incubates

Fledging: 17-21 days; female and male feed young

Migration: non-migrator to partial migrator; will move around to find an abundant food source

Food: insects, fruit, carrion, seeds, nuts; comes to seed feeders, and ground feeders with corn

Compare: Eastern Bluebird (pg. 89) is much smaller and lacks the Jay's white markings and crest. Belted Kingfisher (pg. 99) lacks the vivid blue coloring and black necklace of Jay.

Stan's Notes: Highly intelligent bird, solving problems, gathering food and communicating more than other birds. Will scream like a hawk to scatter birds at a feeder before approaching. Known as the alarm of the forest, screaming at any intruders in the woods. Is known to eat eggs or young birds from nests of other birds. One of the few birds to cache food. Feathers don't contain blue pigment; refracted sunlight casts blue light.

male

female

Belted Kingfisher

Ceryle alcyon

YEAR-ROUND
WINTER

Size: 13" (33 cm)

Male: Large blue bird with white belly. Broad blue gray breast band and a ragged crest that is raised and lowered at will. Large head with a long, thick black bill. A small white spot directly in front of red brown eyes. Black wing tips with splashes of white that flash when flying.

Female: same as male, but with rusty breast band in addition to blue gray band, and rusty flanks

Juvenile: similar to female

Nest: cavity; female and male excavate; 1 brood per year

Eggs: 6-7; white without markings

Incubation: 23-24 days; female and male incubate

Fledging: 23-24 days; female and male feed young

Migration: non-migrator to complete in Texas

Food: small fish

Compare: The Kingfisher is darker blue than Blue Jay (pg. 97) and has a larger, more ragged crest. Larger than the Western Scrub-Jay (pg. 95). Kingfisher is rarely found away from water.

Stan's Notes: Seen perched on branches near the water, it dives headfirst for small fish and returns to a branch to eat. Has a loud machine-gun-like call. Excavates a deep cavity in bank of river or lake. Parents drop dead fish into water, teaching the young to dive. Regurgitates pellets of bone after meals, being unable to pass bones through digestive tract. Mates recognize each other by call.

SUMMER

Purple Gallinule
Porphyrio martinica

Size: 13" (33 cm)

Male: A vibrant blue head, breast and belly with iridescent green back and wings. Yellow-tipped red bill. White undertail. Yellow legs.

Female: same as male

Juvenile: brown version of adult, bronze legs

Nest: ground; female and male build; 1-2 broods per year

Eggs: 6-8; brown with dark markings

Incubation: 22-25 days; female and male incubate

Fledging: 55-60 days; female and male feed young

Migration: complete, to Central and South America

Food: insects, snails, seeds, berries, frogs

Compare: Similar in size to the Coot (pg. 17), which lacks a yellow-tipped red bill. Similar in size to the Moorhen (pg. 15), but differentiated from it by the absence of a white side stripe. Look for the white undertail to help identify the Purple Gallinule.

Stan's Notes: This is one of the most dramatic birds in Texas. Uses its extremely long toes to walk on floating vegetation in freshwater and saltwater marshes, where it hunts for grasshoppers and other insects, grains and frogs. Family groups stay together, with the first brood sometimes helping to raise the second. A summer resident in eastern Texas. Known to wander well north of the state.

non-breeding adult

white juvenile

breeding

molting juvenile

Little Blue Heron
Egretta caerulea

YEAR-ROUND
SUMMER

Size: 24" (60 cm)

Male: Dark slate blue to purple nearly all year. Breeding has several long plumes on crown with a reddish purple head and neck. Dull green legs, feet. Black-tipped blue-gray bill.

Female: same as male

Juvenile: pure white overall, yellowish legs and feet, black-tipped gray bill

Nest: platform; female and male build; 1 brood per year

Eggs: 2-6; light blue without markings

Incubation: 20-23 days; female and male incubate

Fledging: 42-49 days; female and male feed young

Migration: complete to non-migrator, to coastal Texas, Mexico, Central and South America

Food: fish, aquatic insects

Compare: Breeding adult lacks Tricolored's (pg. 105) white belly. Juvenile is confused with the Snowy Egret (pg. 365), which has bright yellow feet, black legs and solid black bill. Breeding Cattle Egret (pg. 361) has orange buff crest, breast and back, red-orange bill.

Stan's Notes: A year-round coastal resident, although much less numerous in winter. Unusual because the young look completely different from adults. All-white young turn blotchy white the first year. By the second year they look like the adult birds. A very slow stalker of prey, feeding in freshwater lakes and rivers, saltwater marshes and wetlands. Nests in large colonies near saltwater sites.

Tricolored Heron
Egretta tricolor

YEAR-ROUND

Size: 26" (66 cm)

Male: Dark blue head, neck and wings contrast with a white belly and neck. Small brown patches at base of neck with lighter brown on lower back. A long, slender yellow bill with a dark tip. Legs yellow to pale green.

Female: same as male

Juvenile: similar to adult, chestnut brown in place of dark blue areas

Nest: platform; female and male build; 1 brood per year

Eggs: 3-6; light blue without markings

Incubation: 21-25 days; female and male incubate

Fledging: 32-35 days; female and male feed young

Migration: non-migrator to partial migrator in Texas

Food: fish, aquatic insects

Compare: Great Blue Heron (pg. 315) is much larger and lacks white undersides. The Little Blue Heron (pg. 103) is slightly smaller and lacks the yellow bill and white belly.

Stan's Notes: A medium-sized heron characterized by its white undersides. Like other herons, Tricolored has declined in numbers due to wetland habitat loss. To hunt, it stands still and waits. Will also chase after small fish. A year-round resident, although much less numerous in the winter. Seen mainly in saltwater marshes and estuaries, but also in freshwater marshes inland. Known to wander as far as Kansas. Colony nester with other herons, one adult always on duty at the nest. Was not hunted for plumes like other herons.

Chipping Sparrow
Spizella passerina

YEAR-ROUND
MIGRATION
WINTER

Size: 5" (13 cm)

Male: Small gray brown sparrow with a clear gray breast, rusty crown and white eyebrows. A black eye line and thin gray black bill. Two faint wing bars.

Female: same as male

Juvenile: similar to adult, has a streaked breast, lacks the rusty crown

Nest: cup; female builds; 2 broods per year

Eggs: 3-5; blue green with brown markings

Incubation: 11-14 days; female incubates

Fledging: 10-12 days; female and male feed young

Migration: complete to non-migrator in Texas

Food: insects, seeds; will come to ground feeders

Compare: Lark Sparrow (pg. 135) is larger and has a white chest and central spot. Song Sparrow (pg. 127) has a heavily streaked chest. The female House Finch (pg. 113) also has a streaked chest.

Stan's Notes: A common garden or yard bird, often seen feeding on dropped seeds beneath feeders. Gathers in large family groups to feed in preparation for migration. Migrates at night in flocks of 20-30 birds. The common name comes from the male's slow "chip" call. Often is just called Chippy. Nest is placed low in dense shrubs and is almost always lined with animal hair. Can be very unafraid of people, allowing you to approach closely before it flies away.

Chimney Swift
Chaetura pelagica

MIGRATION
SUMMER

Size: 5" (13 cm)

Male: Nondescript, swallow-shaped bird, usually seen only in flight. Long, thin brown body with pointed tail and head. Long swept-back wings are longer than body.

Female: same as male

Juvenile: same as adult

Nest: half cup; female and male build; 1 brood per year

Eggs: 4-5; white without markings

Incubation: 19-21 days; female and male incubate

Fledging: 28-30 days; female and male feed young

Migration: complete, to South America

Food: insects caught in air

Compare: The Barn Swallow (pg. 93) has a forked tail unlike the pointed tail of Swift.

Stan's Notes: One of the fastest fliers in the bird world. Spends all day flying, rarely perching. Bathes and drinks by skimming across water surfaces. Unique in-flight twittering call is often heard before bird is seen. Flies in groups, feeding on flying insects nearly 100 feet (30 m) in the air. Often called Flying Cigar due to its pointed body shape. Hundreds will nest and roost in large chimneys, hence the common name. Builds nest with tiny twigs, cementing it with saliva, attaching it to the inside of a chimney or hollow tree.

Pine Siskin
Carduelis pinus

WINTER

Size: 5" (13 cm)

Male: Small brown finch. Heavily streaked back, breast and belly. Yellow wing bars. Yellow at base of tail. Thin bill.

Female: same as male

Juvenile: similar to adult, light yellow tinge over the breast and chin

Nest: modified cup; female constructs; 2 broods per year

Eggs: 3-4; greenish blue with brown markings

Incubation: 12-13 days; female incubates

Fledging: 14-15 days; female and male feed young

Migration: irruptive; moves around the U.S. in search of food

Food: seeds, insects; will come to seed feeders

Compare: Female American Goldfinch (pg. 379) lacks streaks and has white wing bars. Female House Finch (pg. 113) has a streaked chest, but lacks yellow wing bars.

Stan's Notes: A winter finch. Gathers in flocks, moves around the state and visits feeders. Comes to thistle feeders. Travels and breeds in small groups. Male feeds the female during incubation. Juveniles lose yellow tint by late summer of the first year. Builds nest toward the ends of coniferous branches, where needles are dense, helping to conceal. Nests are often only a few feet apart.

male
pg. 345

female

House Finch
Carpodacus mexicanus

YEAR-ROUND

Size: 5" (13 cm)

Female: A plain brown bird with a heavily streaked white chest.

Male: orange red face, chest and rump, brown cap, brown marking behind eyes, brown wings streaked with white, streaked belly

Juvenile: similar to female

Nest: cup, sometimes in cavities; female builds; 2 broods per year

Eggs: 4-5; pale blue, lightly marked

Incubation: 12-14 days; female incubates

Fledging: 15-19 days; female and male feed young

Migration: non-migrator; moves around to find food

Food: seeds, fruit, leaf buds; will visit seed feeders

Compare: Similar to the Pine Siskin (pg. 111), but lacks the yellow wing bars and has a larger bill. Female American Goldfinch (pg. 379) has a clear chest and white wing bars.

Stan's Notes: Very social bird. Visits feeders in small flocks. Likes nesting in hanging flower baskets. Incubating female is fed by the male. Has a loud, cheerful warbling song. Historically it occurred from the Pacific coast to the Rockies, with only a few reaching the eastern side. House Finches that were originally introduced to Long Island, New York, from the western U.S. in the 1940s have since populated the entire eastern U.S. Now found all over the country. Can be the most common bird at your feeders. Suffers from a fatal eye disease that causes the eyes to crust over.

House Wren
Troglodytes aedon

MIGRATION
SUMMER
WINTER

Size: 5" (13 cm)

Male: A small all-brown bird with lighter brown markings on tail and wings. Slightly curved brown bill. Often holds its tail erect.

Female: same as male

Juvenile: same as adult

Nest: cavity; female and male line just about any nest cavity; 2 broods per year

Eggs: 4-6; tan with brown markings

Incubation: 10-13 days; female and male incubate

Fledging: 12-15 days; female and male feed young

Migration: complete, to southern Texas, Mexico

Food: insects

Compare: The Carolina Wren (pg. 117) and Bewick's Wren (pg. 119) are slightly larger and have bold white eyebrows. Wren's long curved bill and long upturned tail distinguishes it from sparrows.

Stan's Notes: A prolific songster, it will sing from dawn until dusk during the mating season. Easily attracted to nest boxes. In spring, the male chooses several prospective nesting cavities and places a few small twigs in each. Female inspects each, chooses one, and finishes the nest building. She will completely fill the nest cavity with uniformly small twigs, then line a small depression at back of cavity with pine needles and grass. Often has trouble fitting long twigs through nest cavity hole. Tries many different directions and approaches until successful.

YEAR-ROUND

Carolina Wren
Thryothorus ludovicianus

Size: 5½" (14 cm)

Male: Warm rusty brown head and back with an orange yellow chest and belly. White throat and a prominent white eye stripe. A short stubby tail, often cocked up.

Female: same as male

Juvenile: same as adult

Nest: cavity; female and male build; 2 broods per year, sometimes 3

Eggs: 4-6; white, sometimes pink or creamy, with brown markings

Incubation: 12-14 days; female incubates

Fledging: 12-14 days; female and male feed young

Migration: non-migrator

Food: insects, fruit, few seeds; visits suet feeders

Compare: Lighter brown than House Wren (pg. 115) and has a bold white eye stripe. Similar to Bewick's Wren (pg. 119), but Carolina Wren has a warm orange yellow chest and belly.

Stan's Notes: A year-round resident in eastern and central Texas. Mates are long-term, remaining together throughout the year in permanent territories. Sings year-round. The male is known to sing up to 40 different song types, singing one song repeatedly before switching to another. Female also sings, resulting in duets. Male often takes over feeding the first brood of young while the female renests. Nests in birdhouses, unusual places such as in mailboxes, bumpers of cars or broken taillights, or in nearly any other cavity. Found in brushy yards or woodlands.

Bewick's Wren
Thryomanes bewickii

YEAR-ROUND

Size: 5½" (14 cm)

Male: Brown cap, back, wings and tail. Gray chest and belly. White chin and eyebrows. Long tail with white spots on edges is cocked and flits sideways. Pointed down-curved bill.

Female: same as male

Juvenile: similar to adult

Nest: cavity; female and male build nest in woodpecker hole or nest box; 2-3 broods a year

Eggs: 4-8; white with brown markings

Incubation: 12-14 days; female incubates

Fledging: 10-14 days; female and male feed young

Migration: non-migrator

Food: insects, seeds

Compare: House Wren (pg. 115) is slightly smaller and lacks the obvious white eyebrow marks and white spots on tail. Similar to Carolina Wren (pg. 117), but the Bewick's Wren has a gray chest.

Stan's Notes: A common wren of backyards and gardens. Insects make up 97 percent of its diet, with plant seeds composing the rest. Competes with House Wrens for nesting cavities. Male will choose nesting cavities and start to build nests using small uniform-sized sticks. Female will make the final selection of a nest site and finish building. Begins breeding in March and April. Has 2-3 broods per year. Male feeds female while she incubates. Average size territory per pair is 5 acres (2 ha), which they defend all year long. The brown (Eastern) and grayish brown (Western) Bewick's both occur in Texas. Map reflects the combined range.

male pg. 253

female

pink-sided

Oregon female

Dark-eyed Junco
Junco hyemalis

WINTER

Size: 5½" (14 cm)

Female: A round, dark-eyed bird with tan-to-brown chest, head and back. White belly. Ivory-to-pink bill. Since the outermost tail feathers are white, tail appears as a white V in flight.

Male: same as female, only slate gray to charcoal

Juvenile: similar to female, but has a streaked breast and head

Nest: cup; female and male construct; 2 broods per year

Eggs: 3-5; white with reddish brown markings

Incubation: 12-13 days; female incubates

Fledging: 10-13 days; male and female feed young

Migration: complete, to Texas

Food: seeds, insects; will come to seed feeders

Compare: Rarely confused with any other bird. Small flocks feed under bird feeders in winter.

Stan's Notes: Several junco species have now been combined into one, simply called Dark-eyed Junco (see lower insets). Spends the winter in the foothills and plains after snowmelt. Nests in a wide variety of wooded habitats in April and May. Adheres to a rigid social hierarchy, with dominant birds chasing less dominant birds. Look for its white outer tail feathers flashing while in flight. Most comfortable on the ground, juncos "double-scratch" with both feet to expose seeds and insects. Eats many weed seeds. Usually seen on the ground in small flocks. Doesn't nest in Texas.

female

male pg. 83

Indigo Bunting
Passerina cyanea

MIGRATION
SUMMER

Size: 5½" (14 cm)

Female: Light brown finch-like bird. Faint streaking on a light tan chest. Wings have a very faint blue cast with indistinct wing bars.

Male: vibrant blue finch-like bird, scattered dark markings on wings and tail

Juvenile: similar to female

Nest: cup; female builds; 2 broods per year

Eggs: 3-4; pale blue without markings

Incubation: 12-13 days; female incubates

Fledging: 10-11 days; female feeds young

Migration: complete, to Mexico, Central America and South America

Food: insects, seeds, fruit; will visit seed feeders

Compare: Female Blue Grosbeak (pg. 139) is larger and has 2 tan wing bars. The female Indigo Bunting is similar to female finches. Female American Goldfinch (pg. 379) has white wing bars. Female House Finch (pg. 113) has a heavily streaked chest.

Stan's Notes: A secretive bird, usually only the male buntings are seen. Males often sing from treetops to attract mates. Will come to feeders in the spring before insects are plentiful. Mostly seen along woodland edges, feeding on insects. Migrates during the night in flocks of 5-10 birds. A late migrant, males return before the females and juveniles. Juveniles move to within a mile from birth site.

Cliff Swallow

Petrochelidon pyrrhonota

SUMMER

Size: 5½" (14 cm)

Male: A uniquely patterned swallow with a dark back, wings and cap. Distinctive tan-to-rust rump, cheeks and forehead.

Female: same as male

Juvenile: similar to adult, lacks distinct patterning

Nest: gourd-shaped, made of mud; the male and female build; 1-2 broods per year

Eggs: 3-6; pale white with brown markings

Incubation: 14-16 days; male and female incubate

Fledging: 21-24 days; female and male feed young

Migration: complete, to South America

Food: insects

Compare: Smaller than Barn Swallow (pg. 93), which has a distinctive, deeply forked tail and blue back and wings.

Stan's Notes: Common and widespread swallow species in Texas during summer. Common around bridges (especially bridges over water) and rural housing (especially in open country close to cliffs). Constructs a gourd-shaped nest with a funnel-like entrance pointing down. Colony nester, with many nests lined up beneath eaves of buildings or under cliff overhangs. Will carry balls of mud up to a mile to construct its nest. Many of the colony return to the same nest sites each year. Not unusual to have two broods per season. If the number of nests beneath eaves becomes a problem, wait until after young have left nests to hose off mud.

WINTER

Song Sparrow
Melospiza melodia

Size: 5-6" (13-15 cm)

Male: Common brown sparrow with heavy dark streaks on breast coalescing into a central dark spot.

Female: same as male

Juvenile: similar to adult, finely streaked breast, lacks a central spot

Nest: cup; female builds; 2 broods per year

Eggs: 3-4; pale blue to green with reddish brown markings

Incubation: 12-14 days; female incubates

Fledging: 9-12 days; female and male feed young

Migration: complete, to Texas

Food: insects, seeds; rarely visits seed feeders

Compare: Similar to other brown sparrows. Look for a heavily streaked chest with central dark spot.

Stan's Notes: Many Song Sparrow subspecies or varieties, but dark central spot carries through each variant. While the female builds another nest for a second brood, the male sparrow often takes over feeding the young. Returns to a similar area each year, defending a small territory by singing from thick shrubs. A common host of the Brown-headed Cowbird. Ground feeders, look for them to scratch simultaneously with both feet to expose seeds. Unlike many other sparrow species, Song Sparrows rarely flock together. A constant songster, repeating its loud, clear song every couple minutes. Song varies in structure, but is basically the same from region to region.

House Sparrow
Passer domesticus

Size: 6" (15 cm)

Male: Medium sparrow-like bird with large black spot on throat extending down to the chest. Brown back and single white wing bars. A gray belly and crown.

Female: slightly smaller than the male, light brown, lacks the throat patch and single wing bars

Juvenile: similar to female

Nest: domed cup nest, within cavity; female and male build; 2-3 broods per year

Eggs: 4-6; white with brown markings

Incubation: 10-12 days; female incubates

Fledging: 14-17 days; female and male feed young

Migration: non-migrator; moves around to find food

Food: seeds, insects, fruit; comes to seed feeders

Compare: Lacks the rusty crown of Chipping Sparrow (pg. 107). Look for male House Sparrow's black bib. Female has a clear breast and no marking on head (cap).

Stan's Notes: One of the first bird songs heard in cities in spring. Familiar city bird, nearly always in small flocks. Introduced from Europe to Central Park, New York, in 1850. Now found throughout North America. These birds are not really sparrows, but members of the Weaver Finch family, characterized by their large, oversized domed nests. Constructs a nest containing scraps of plastic, paper and whatever else is available. An aggressive bird that will kill the young of other birds in order to take over a cavity.

winter pg. 259

breeding

Least Sandpiper
Calidris minutilla

YEAR-ROUND
MIGRATION
WINTER

Size: 6" (15 cm)

Male: Breeding plumage has a golden brown head and back. White eyebrows and belly. Dull yellow legs. Short, down-curved black bill.

Female: same as male

Juvenile: similar to winter adult, but buff brown and lacking the breast band

Nest: ground; male and female construct; 1 brood per year

Eggs: 3-4; olive with dark markings

Incubation: 19-23 days; male and female incubate

Fledging: 25-28 days; male and female feed young

Migration: complete to non-migrator, to Texas, Mexico and Central America

Food: aquatic and terrestrial insects, seeds

Compare: The smallest of sandpipers. The yellow legs differentiate it from other tiny sandpipers, and the short, thin, down-curved bill helps to identify.

Stan's Notes: This is a tiny, tame sandpiper that can be approached without scaring. The smallest of peeps (sandpipers), it nests on the tundra in northern regions of Canada and Alaska. Prefers the grassy flats of saltwater and freshwater ponds. Its yellow legs can be hard to see in water, poor light or if covered with mud.

131

female

male pg. 37

non-breeding
male

Lark Bunting
Calamospiza melanocorys

SUMMER WINTER

Size: 6½" (16 cm)

Female: Brown bird with heavily streaked chest and a white belly. Black vertical line on each side of white chin. May have a central dark spot on the chest. Faint white eyebrows.

Male: black bird with a large broad head, white wing patches and large bluish gray bill

Juvenile: similar to adult of the same sex

Nest: cup; female builds; 1-2 broods per year

Eggs: 4-6; pale blue with markings

Incubation: 11-13 days; female and male incubate

Fledging: 8-12 days; female and male feed young

Migration: complete, to most of Texas, Mexico

Food: insects, seeds

Compare: Appears similar to open country sparrows. The female Red-winged Blackbird (pg. 155) lacks the white belly and chin.

Stan's Notes: Common in the dry plains and sagebrush regions of the state. Has short rounded wings. Flying with shallow wing beats, the male flashes white wing patches. Male takes to air to display to female, setting its wings in a V position and floating back, rocking like a butterfly, singing a most amazing song. Song is like the song of Old World larks, hence the common name. Will flock in fall with hundreds, if not thousands, of other Lark Buntings for migration.

Lark Sparrow
Chondestes grammacus

YEAR-ROUND
SUMMER

Size: 6½" (16 cm)

Male: All-brown bird with unique rust red, white and black head pattern. A white breast with a central black spot. Gray rump and white edges to gray tail, as seen in flight.

Female: same as male

Juvenile: similar to adult, no rust red on head

Nest: cup, on the ground; female builds; 1 brood per year

Eggs: 3-6; pale white with brown markings

Incubation: 10-12 days; male and female incubate

Fledging: 10-12 days; female and male feed young

Migration: non-migrator to complete in Texas

Food: seeds, insects

Compare: Larger than Chipping Sparrow (pg. 107), which has a similar rusty color on head, but lacks Lark's white breast and central spot.

Stan's Notes: One of the larger sparrow species and one of the best songsters, also well known for its courtship strutting, chasing and lark-like flight pattern (rapid wing beats with tail spread). A bird of open fields, pastures and prairies, found almost anywhere. Very common during migration, when large flocks congregate. Will use nest for several years if first brood is successful.

white-striped

tan-striped

White-throated Sparrow
Zonotrichia albicollis

MIGRATION
WINTER

Size: 6-7" (15-18 cm)

Male: A brown bird with gray tan chest and belly. Small yellow spot between the eyes (lore). Distinctive white or tan throat patch. White or tan stripes alternate with black stripes on crown. Color of the throat patch and crown stripes match.

Female: same as male

Juvenile: similar to adult, gray throat and eyebrows with heavily streaked chest

Nest: cup; female builds; 1 brood per year

Eggs: 4-6; color varies from greenish to bluish to creamy white with red brown markings

Incubation: 11-14 days; female incubates

Fledging: 10-12 days; female and male feed young

Migration: complete, to Texas and Mexico

Food: insects, seeds, fruit; visits ground feeders

Compare: Song Sparrow (pg. 127) has a central spot on the breast and lacks a striped pattern on the head.

Stan's Notes: There are two color variations (polymorphic) of the White-throated Sparrow: white-striped or tan-striped. Studies have indicated the white-striped adults tend to mate with the tan-striped birds. No indication why. A winter resident that is more abundant during migration, when it can be seen at ground feeders. Nests are built on the ground underneath small trees in bogs and coniferous forests. Doesn't nest in Texas.

male pg. 85

female

Blue Grosbeak
Passerina caerulea

MIGRATION
SUMMER

Size: 7" (18 cm)

Female: Overall brown with darker wings and tail. Two tan wing bars. Large gray-to-silver bill.

Male: blue bird with 2 chestnut wing bars, a large gray-to-silver bill, black around base of bill

Juvenile: similar to female

Nest: cup; female builds; 1-2 broods per year

Eggs: 3-6; pale blue without markings

Incubation: 11-12 days; female incubates

Fledging: 9-10 days; female and male feed young

Migration: complete, to Mexico and Central America

Food: insects, seeds; will come to seed feeders

Compare: Female Indigo Bunting (pg. 123) is similar, but lacks the tan wing bars and is lighter in color overall.

Stan's Notes: This grosbeak returns to Texas by early May. It has expanded northward with overall populations increasing over the past 30-40 years. A bird of semi-open habitats such as overgrown fields, riversides, woodland edges and fencerows. Frequently seen twitching and spreading its tail. First-year males show only some blue, obtaining the full complement of blue feathers in the second winter. Visits seed feeders.

male pg. 5

female

Brown-headed Cowbird
Molothrus ater

YEAR-ROUND

Size: 7½" (19 cm)

Female: Dull brown bird with no obvious markings. Pointed, sharp gray bill.

Male: glossy black bird, chocolate brown head

Juvenile: similar to female, only dull gray color and a streaked chest

Nest: no nest; lays eggs in nests of other birds

Eggs: 5-7; white with brown markings

Incubation: 10-13 days; host bird incubates eggs

Fledging: 10-11 days; host birds feed young

Migration: non-migrator in Texas

Food: insects, seeds; will come to seed feeders

Compare: Female Red-winged Blackbird (pg. 155) is slightly larger and has white eyebrows and a streaked chest. European Starling (pg. 3) has speckles and a shorter tail.

Stan's Notes: A member of the blackbird family. Of approximately 750 species of parasitic birds worldwide, this is the only parasitic bird in the state, laying eggs in host birds' nests, leaving others to raise its young. Cowbirds are known to have laid eggs in nests of over 200 species of birds. Some birds reject cowbird eggs, but most incubate them and raise the young, even to the exclusion of their own. Look for warblers and other birds feeding young birds twice their own size. At one time cowbirds followed bison to feed on insects attracted to the animals.

1 year old

Cedar Waxwing
Bombycilla cedrorum

WINTER

Size: 7½" (19 cm)

Male: Very sleek-looking gray-to-brown bird with pointed crest, light yellow belly and bandit-like black mask. Tip of tail is bright yellow and the tips of wings look as if they have been dipped in red wax.

Female: same as male

Juvenile: grayish with a heavily streaked chest, lacks red wing tips, black mask and sleek look

Nest: cup; female and male construct; 1 brood per year, occasionally 2

Eggs: 4-6; pale blue with brown markings

Incubation: 10-12 days; female incubates

Fledging: 14-18 days; female and male feed young

Migration: complete to partial migrator; moves to Texas to find food

Food: cedar cones, fruit, insects

Compare: Female Cardinal (pg. 159) has a large red bill. Look for Waxwing's black mask and yellow-tipped tail to help identify.

Stan's Notes: The name is derived from its red wax-like wing tips and preference for eating small blueberry-like cones of the cedar. Mostly seen in flocks, moving from area to area, looking for berries. Wanders in winter to find available food supplies. During summer, before berries are abundant, it feeds on insects. Spends most of its time at the tops of tall trees. Listen for the very high-pitched "sreee" whistling sounds it constantly makes. Obtains mask after first year and red wing tips after second year. Doesn't nest in Texas.

Horned Lark
Eremophila alpestris

YEAR-ROUND

Size: 7-8" (18-20 cm)

Male: A sleek tan-to-brown bird. Black necklace with a yellow chin and black bill. Two tiny "horns" on the top of head can be difficult to see. A dark tail with white outer feathers, noticeable in flight.

Female: duller than male, "horns" less noticeable

Juvenile: lacks the black markings and yellow chin, doesn't form "horns" until second year

Nest: ground; female builds; 2-3 broods per year

Eggs: 3-4; gray with brown markings

Incubation: 11-12 days; female incubates

Fledging: 9-12 days; female and male feed young

Migration: non-migrator in Texas

Food: seeds, insects

Compare: Smaller than Meadowlark (pg. 405), which shares the black necklace and yellow chin. Look for the black marks in front of eyes.

Stan's Notes: The only true lark native to North America. A year-round resident, moving about in winter to find food. Horned Larks are birds of open ground. Common in rural areas, frequently seen in large flocks. Population increased in North America over the past 100 years due to land clearing for farming. May have up to three broods per year because they get such an early start. Male performs a fluttering courtship flight high in the air while singing a high-pitched song. Female performs a fluttering distraction display if nest is disturbed. Can renest about a week after brood fledges. The name "Lark" comes from the Middle English word *laverock*, or "a lark."

male pg. 343

female

Black-headed Grosbeak

Pheucticus melanocephalus

MIGRATION
SUMMER

Size: 8" (20 cm)

Female: Appears like an overgrown sparrow. Overall brown with a lighter breast and belly. Large two-toned bill. Prominent white eyebrows. Yellow wing linings, as seen in flight.

Male: burnt orange chest, neck and rump, black head, tail and wings with irregular-shaped white wing patches, large bill with upper bill darker than lower

Juvenile: similar to adult of the same sex

Nest: cup; female builds; 1 brood per year

Eggs: 3-4; pale green or bluish, brown markings

Incubation: 11-13 days; female and male incubate

Fledging: 11-13 days; female and male feed young

Migration: complete, to Mexico, Central America and South America

Food: seeds, insects, fruit; comes to seed feeders

Compare: Female House Finch (pg. 113) is smaller, has more streaking on the chest and the bill isn't as large. Look for female Grosbeak's unusual bicolored bill.

Stan's Notes: A cosmopolitan bird that nests in a wide variety of habitats. Both the male and female sing and will aggressively defend the nest against intruders. Song is very similar to American Robin's, making it hard to tell them apart by song. Populations increasing in Texas and across the U.S.

winter

breeding

Spotted Sandpiper
Actitis macularius

MIGRATION
WINTER

Size: 8" (20 cm)

Male: Olive brown back. Long bill and long dull yellow legs. White line over eyes. Breeding plumage has black spots on a white chest and belly. Winter has a clear chest and belly.

Female: same as male

Juvenile: similar to winter adult, with a darker bill

Nest: ground; female and male build; 2 broods per year

Eggs: 3-4; brownish with brown markings

Incubation: 20-24 days; male incubates

Fledging: 17-21 days; male feeds young

Migration: complete migrator, to the southern half of Texas, Mexico, Central and South America

Food: aquatic insects

Compare: The Killdeer (pg. 169) has 2 black bands around neck. Look for the Sandpiper to bob its tail up and down while standing. Look for the breeding Spotted Sandpiper's black spots extending from chest to belly.

Stan's Notes: One of the few shorebirds that will dive underwater if pursued. Able to fly straight up out of the water. Flies with wings held in a cup-like arc, rarely lifting them above a horizontal plane. Constantly bobs its tail while standing and walks as if delicately balanced. Female mates with multiple males and lays eggs in up to five different nests. Male incubates and cares for young. Dramatic plumage change from breeding to winter. Lacks black spots on the chest and belly in winter.

winter pg. 273

breeding

Sanderling
Calidris alba

YEAR-ROUND
MIGRATION

Size: 8" (20 cm)

Male: Breeding season (April to August) plumage has a rusty head, chest and back with white belly. Black legs and bill.

Female: same as male

Juvenile: spotty black on the head and back, a white belly, black legs and bill

Nest: ground; male builds; 1-2 broods per year

Eggs: 3-4; greenish olive with brown markings

Incubation: 24-30 days; male and female incubate

Fledging: 16-17 days; female and male feed young

Migration: complete to non-migrator, to coastal Texas, Mexico, Central and South America

Food: insects

Compare: The breeding plumage Spotted Sandpiper (pg. 149) is the same size, but has black spots on its chest.

Stan's Notes: One of the most common shorebirds in Texas, but mostly seen in gray winter plumage from August to April. Can be seen in groups on sandy beaches, running out with each retreating wave to feed. Look for a flash of white on wings when it is in flight. Occasionally the female will mate with several males (polyandry), resulting in males and the female incubating separate nests. Both sexes will perform a distraction display if threatened. Nests on the Arctic tundra. Rests by standing on one leg (see inset), tucking the other leg into its belly feathers. Will often hop away on one leg, moving away from pedestrians on the beach.

Cactus Wren
Campylorhynchus brunneicapillus

YEAR-ROUND

Size: 8½" (22 cm)

Male: A large round-bodied wren with a long tail and a large, slightly downward curving bill. Bold white eyebrows and a chestnut brown crown. Many dark spots on upper breast to throat, often forming a central dark patch.

Female: same as male

Juvenile: similar to adult, shorter bill, lacks a spotty dark patch on breast

Nest: covered cup, domed or ball-shaped; female and male build; 2-3 broods per year

Eggs: 3-4; pale white to pink with brown marks

Incubation: 14-16 days; female incubates

Fledging: 19-23 days; female and male feed young

Migration: non-migrator

Food: insects, fruit, seeds; comes to seed feeders and water elements

Compare: The Curve-billed Thrasher (pg. 289) has a longer bill. Look for the Wren's prominent white eyebrows to help identify.

Stan's Notes: Our largest wren. Backyard bird with a loud "krr-krr-krr-krr-krr" or "cha-cha-cha-cha." Male crouches, extends wings, fans tail and growls to female during courtship. Pairs stay together all, defending territory. Builds a large nest usually in cholla or cactus, lining the chamber with grasses and feathers. Male builds another nest while female incubates first clutch of eggs. After the second brood fledges, roosts in nest during non-breeding season.

male pg. 9

female

Red-winged Blackbird
Agelaius phoeniceus

YEAR-ROUND

Size: 8½" (22 cm)

Female: Heavily streaked brown bird with a pointed brown bill and white eyebrows.

Male: jet black bird with red and yellow patches on upper wings, pointed black bill

Juvenile: same as female

Nest: cup; female builds; 2-3 broods per year

Eggs: 3-4; bluish green with brown markings

Incubation: 10-12 days; female incubates

Fledging: 11-14 days; female and male feed young

Migration: non-migrator to partial migrator

Food: seeds, insects; will come to seed feeders

Compare: Larger than female Brown-headed Cowbird (pg. 141) and smaller than female Yellow-headed Blackbird (pg. 165), both of which lack white eyebrows and streaks on chest.

Stan's Notes: One of the most widespread and numerous birds in the state. It is a sure sign of spring when the Red-winged Blackbirds return to the marshes. Flocks of up to 100,000 birds have been reported. Males return before the females and defend territories by singing from tops of surrounding vegetation. Males repeat call from the tops of cattails while showing off their red and yellow wing bars (epaulets). Females choose mate and usually will nest over shallow water in thick stands of cattails. Red-wingeds feed mostly on seeds in fall and spring, switching to insects during summer.

male pg. 7

female

Eastern
female

Spotted Towhee
Pipilo maculatus

YEAR-ROUND
WINTER

Size: 8½" (22 cm)

Female: A brown head, dirty red-brown sides and a white belly. Multiple white spots on wings and sides. Long black tail with a white tip. Rich red eyes.

Male: mostly black, lacking the brown head

Juvenile: brown with a heavily streaked chest

Nest: cup; female builds; 1-2 broods per year

Eggs: 3-5; white with brown markings

Incubation: 12-14 days; female and male incubate

Fledging: 10-12 days; female and male feed young

Migration: partial migrator to non-migrator

Food: seeds, fruit, insects

Compare: Smaller than American Robin (pg. 285).

Stan's Notes: The Spotted Towhee and Eastern Towhee were once considered a single species called Rufous-sided Towhee. Found in a variety of habitats, from thick brush and chaparral to suburban backyards. Usually heard noisily scratching through dead leaves on the ground for food. Over 70 percent of its diet is plant material. Eats more insects during spring and summer. Well known to retreat from danger by walking away rather than taking to flight. Nest is nearly always on the ground under bushes, but away from where the male perches to sing. Begins breeding in April. Lays eggs in May. After the breeding season, moves to higher elevations. Song and plumage vary geographically and aren't well studied or understood.

male pg. 351

female

juvenile

YEAR-ROUND

Northern Cardinal
Cardinalis cardinalis

Size: 8-9" (20-22.5 cm)

Female: Buff brown bird with tinges of red on crest and wings, a black mask and large red bill.

Male: red bird with a black mask extending from face down to chin and throat, large red bill and crest

Juvenile: same as female, but with a blackish gray bill

Nest: cup; female builds; 2-3 broods per year

Eggs: 3-4; bluish white with brown markings

Incubation: 12-13 days; female and male incubate

Fledging: 9-10 days; female and male feed young

Migration: non-migrator

Food: seeds, insects, fruit; comes to seed feeders

Compare: Cedar Waxwing (pg. 143) has a small dark bill. Female Cardinal appears similar to the juvenile Cardinal, but the juvenile has a dark bill. Look for the bright red bill of the female Cardinal.

Stan's Notes: A familiar backyard bird. Look for the male feeding female during courtship. Male feeds young of the first brood by himself while female builds second nest. The name comes from the Latin word *cardinalis*, which means "important." Very territorial in spring, it will fight its own reflection in a window. Non-territorial during winter, gathering in small flocks of up to 20 birds. Both the female and male sing and can be heard anytime of year. Listen for its "whata-cheer-cheer-cheer" territorial call in spring.

female

male

SUMMER

Common Nighthawk
Chordeiles minor

Size: 9" (22.5 cm)

Male: A camouflaged brown and white bird with white chin. A distinctive white band across wings and the tail, seen only in flight.

Female: similar to male, but with tan chin, lacks the white tail band

Juvenile: similar to female

Nest: no nest; lays eggs on the ground, usually on rocks, or on rooftop; 1 brood per year

Eggs: 2; cream with lavender markings

Incubation: 19-20 days; female and male incubate

Fledging: 20-21 days; female and male feed young

Migration: complete, to South America

Food: insects caught in air

Compare: Much larger than Chimney Swift (pg. 109). Look for the obvious white wing band of Nighthawk in flight, and the characteristic flap-flap-flap-glide flight pattern.

Stan's Notes: Usually only seen flying at dusk or after sunset, but not uncommon for it to be sitting on a fence post, sleeping during the day. A very noisy bird, repeating a "peenting" call during flight. Alternates slow wing beats with bursts of quick wing beats. Prolific insect eater. Prefers gravel rooftops for nesting in cities and nests on the ground in country. Male's distinctive springtime mating ritual is a steep diving flight terminated with a loud popping noise. One of the first birds to migrate each fall, starting in August. A summer resident throughout Texas.

Burrowing Owl
Athene cunicularia

YEAR-ROUND
SUMMER
WINTER

Size: 9½" (24 cm); up to 21-inch wingspan

Male: A brown owl with bold white spots, white belly and very long legs. Yellow eyes.

Female: same as male

Juvenile: same as adult, but belly is brown

Nest: cavity, former underground mammal den; female and male line den; 1 brood per year

Eggs: 6-11; white without markings

Incubation: 21-28 days; female incubates

Fledging: 25-28 days; female and male feed young

Migration: non-migrator to partial migrator in Texas

Food: insects, mammals, lizards, birds

Compare: Eastern Screech-Owl (pg. 283) is slightly smaller and has ear tufts. Burrowing Owl is less than half the size of Great Horned Owl (pg. 237), which has feather tuft "horns." Burrowing spends most of its time on the ground unlike tree-loving Great Horned.

Stan's Notes: An owl of fields, open backyards, golf courses and airports. Nests in small family units or in small colonies. Takes over the underground dens of mammals, occasionally widening its den by kicking dirt backward. Lines den with cow pies, horse dung, grass and feathers. Some people have had success attracting these owls to their backyards by creating artificial dens. Often seen in the day, standing or sleeping around den entrance. Male brings food to incubating female, often moving family to a new den when young are just a few weeks old. Will bob head up and down while doing deep knee bends when agitated or threatened.

163

male pg. 11

female

Yellow-headed Blackbird
Xanthocephalus xanthocephalus

MIGRATION
WINTER

Size: 9-11" (22.5-28 cm)

Female: A large brown bird with a dull yellow head and chest. Slightly smaller than male.

Male: black bird with a lemon yellow head, chest and nape of neck, black mask and gray bill, white wing patches

Juvenile: similar to female

Nest: cup; female builds; 2 broods per year

Eggs: 3-5; greenish white with brown markings

Incubation: 11-13 days; female incubates

Fledging: 9-12 days; female feeds young

Migration: complete, to western parts of Texas, Mexico

Food: insects, seeds; will come to ground feeders

Compare: Larger than female Red-winged Blackbird (pg. 155), which has white eyebrows and a streaked chest.

Stan's Notes: Usually heard before seen, Yellow-headed Blackbird has a low, hoarse, raspy or metallic call. Nests in deep water marshes unlike its cousin, the Red-winged Blackbird, which prefers shallow water. The male gives an impressive mating display, flying with head drooped and feet and tail pointing down while steadily beating its wings. The female incubates alone and feeds 3-5 young. Young keep low and out of sight for as many as three weeks before starting to fly. Migrates in flocks of up to 200 with other blackbirds. Flocks made up mainly of males return first in early April; females return later. Most colonies consist of 20-100 nests.

Brown Thrasher
Toxostoma rufum

YEAR-ROUND
SUMMER
WINTER

Size: 11" (28 cm)

Male: A rusty red bird with long tail and heavily streaked breast and belly. Two white wing bars. Long curved bill. Bright yellow eyes.

Female: same as male

Juvenile: same as adult, but eye color is grayish

Nest: cup; female and male construct; 2 broods per year

Eggs: 4-5; pale blue with brown markings

Incubation: 11-14 days; female and male incubate

Fledging: 10-13 days; female and male feed young

Migration: complete to non-migrator in Texas

Food: insects, fruit

Compare: The Curve-billed Thrasher (pg. 289) is the same size, but Brown Thrasher is rusty red and has a smaller, less curved bill. Slightly larger in size and similar in shape to the American Robin (pg. 285) and Gray Catbird (pg. 277), but Brown Thrasher has a streaked chest, rusty color and yellow eyes.

Stan's Notes: A prodigious songster, often in thick shrubs where it sings deliberate musical phrases, repeating each twice. Male has the largest documented song repertoire of all North American birds, with over 1,100 song types. Often seen quickly flying or running in and out of dense shrubs. Noisy feeding due to habit of turning over leaves, small rocks and branches. This bird is more abundant in the central Great Plains than anywhere else in North America.

Killdeer
Charadrius vociferus

YEAR-ROUND

Size: 11" (28 cm)

Male: An upland shorebird that has 2 black bands around the neck like a necklace. A brown back and white belly. Bright reddish orange rump, visible in flight.

Female: same as male

Juvenile: similar to adult, with 1 neck band

Nest: ground; male builds; 2 broods per year

Eggs: 3-5; tan with brown markings

Incubation: 24-28 days; male and female incubate

Fledging: 25 days; male and female lead their young to food

Migration: non-migrator in Texas

Food: insects

Compare: The Spotted Sandpiper (pg. 149) is found around water and lacks the 2 neck bands of the Killdeer.

Stan's Notes: The only shorebird with two black neck bands. It is known for its broken wing impression, which draws intruders away from nest. Once clear of the nest, the Killdeer takes flight. Nests are only a slight depression in a gravel area, often very difficult to see. Young look like yellow cotton balls on stilts when first hatched, but quickly molt to appear similar to parents. Able to follow parents and peck for insects soon after birth. Is technically classified as a shorebird, but doesn't live at the shore. Often found in vacant fields or along railroads. Has a very distinctive "kill-deer" call.

American Kestrel
Falco sparverius

YEAR-ROUND
WINTER

Size: 10-12" (25-30 cm); up to 2-foot wingspan

Male: Rusty brown back and tail. A white breast with dark spots. Double black vertical lines on white face. Blue gray wings. Distinctive wide black band with a white edge on tip of rusty tail.

Female: similar to male, but slightly larger, has rusty brown wings and dark bands on tail

Juvenile: same as adult of the same sex

Nest: cavity; doesn't build a nest within; 1 brood per year

Eggs: 4-5; white with brown markings

Incubation: 29-31 days; male and female incubate

Fledging: 30-31 days; female and male feed young

Migration: non-migrator to partial migrator in Texas

Food: insects, small mammals and birds, reptiles

Compare: Similar to other falcons. Look for 2 vertical black stripes on the Kestrel's face. No other small bird of prey has a rusty back and tail.

Stan's Notes: A falcon that was once called Sparrow Hawk due to its small size. Could be called Grasshopper Hawk because it eats many grasshoppers. Hovers close to roads before diving for prey. Adapts quickly to a wooden nesting box. Has pointed swept-back wings, seen in flight. Perches nearly upright. Unusual raptor in that males and females have quite different markings. Watch for them to pump their tails up and down after landing on perches.

yellow-shafted female

red-shafted male

red-shafted female

Northern Flicker
Colaptes auratus

YEAR-ROUND WINTER

Size: 12" (30 cm)

Male: Brown and black woodpecker with a large white rump patch visible only when flying. Black necklace above a speckled breast. Red spot on nape of neck and black mustache.

Female: same as male, but lacking a black mustache

Juvenile: same as adult of the same sex

Nest: cavity; female and male excavate; 1 brood per year

Eggs: 5-8; white without markings

Incubation: 11-14 days; female and male incubate

Fledging: 25-28 days; female and male feed young

Migration: non-migrator to partial migrator in Texas

Food: insects, especially ants and beetles

Compare: Male Yellow-bellied Sapsucker (pg. 45) is smaller and has a red chin. The male Red-bellied Woodpecker (pg. 51) has a red cap and lacks a mustache. Flickers are the only brown-backed woodpeckers in Texas.

Stan's Notes: This is the only woodpecker to regularly feed on the ground. Preferring ants and beetles, it produces an antacid saliva to neutralize the acidic defense of ants. Male usually selects nest site, taking up to 12 days to excavate. Some have had success attracting flickers to nest boxes stuffed with sawdust. Yellow-shafted variety has golden yellow wing linings and tails. Male yellow-shafteds have black mustaches; male red-shafteds have red mustaches. Hybrids between varieties occur in the Great Plains, where ranges overlap. Undulates deeply in flight while giving loud "wacka-wacka" calls.

Mourning Dove
Zenaida macroura

YEAR-ROUND

Size: 12" (30 cm)

Male: Smooth fawn-colored dove with gray patch on the head. Iridescent pink, green around neck. A single black spot behind and below eyes. Black spots on wings and tail. Pointed wedge-shaped tail with white edges.

Female: similar to male, lacking iridescent pink and green neck feathers

Juvenile: spotted and streaked

Nest: platform; female and male build; 2 broods per year

Eggs: 2; white without markings

Incubation: 13-14 days; male and female incubate, the male during day, female at night

Fledging: 12-14 days; female and male feed young

Migration: non-migrator to partial migrator; will move around to find food

Food: seeds; will visit seed and ground feeders

Compare: The Eurasian Collared-Dove (pg. 297) has a black collar. Similar to the White-winged Dove (pg. 291), but lacking a white edge.

Stan's Notes: Name comes from its mournful cooing. A ground feeder, bobbing its head as it walks. One of the few birds to drink without lifting its head, same as Rock Pigeon. Parents feed young (squab) a regurgitated liquid called crop-milk for the first few days of life. Flimsy platform nest of twigs often falls apart during a storm. Wind rushing through wing feathers during flight creates a characteristic whistling sound.

winter

breeding

Pied-billed Grebe
Podilymbus podiceps

YEAR-ROUND
WINTER

Size: 13" (33 cm)

Male: Small brown water bird with a black chin and black ring around a thick, chicken-like ivory bill. Puffy white patch under the tail. Has an unmarked brown bill during winter (September to February).

Female: same as male

Juvenile: paler than adult, with white spots and gray chest, belly and bill

Nest: floating platform; female and male build; 1 brood per year

Eggs: 5-7; bluish white without markings

Incubation: 22-24 days; female and male incubate

Fledging: 22-24 days; female and male feed young

Migration: complete to non-migrator in Texas

Food: crayfish, aquatic insects, fish

Compare: Look for a puffy white patch under the tail and thick, chicken-like bill to help identify.

Stan's Notes: Common resident grebe, often seen diving for food. Slowly sinks like a submarine if disturbed. Sinks without diving by quickly compressing feathers to force air out. Was called Hell-diver because of the length of time it can stay submerged. Can surface far from where it went under. Very sensitive to pollution. Adapted well to life on water, with short wings, lobed toes, and legs set close to rear of body. While swimming is easy, it is very awkward on land. Builds nest on a floating mat in water. "Grebe" probably came from the Old English *krib*, meaning "crest," a reference to the crested head plumes of many grebes, especially during breeding season.

male pg. 61

female

Bufflehead
Bucephala albeola

WINTER

Size: 13-15" (33-38 cm)

Female: Brownish gray duck with dark brown head. White patch on cheek, just behind eyes.

Male: striking black and white duck with a head that shines green purple in sunlight, large white bonnet-like patch on back of head

Juvenile: similar to female

Nest: cavity; female lines old woodpecker cavity; 1 brood per year

Eggs: 8-10; ivory to olive without markings

Incubation: 29-31 days; female incubates

Fledging: 50-55 days; female leads young to food

Migration: complete, to Texas, Mexico, Central America

Food: aquatic insects

Compare: Slightly smaller than female Lesser Scaup (pg. 201), which has a white patch at the base of bill unlike female Bufflehead's white patch on the cheek.

Stan's Notes: Common diving duck that travels with other ducks. Seen during migration and throughout winter, arriving in the state late in August. Found on rivers and lakes. Nests in old woodpecker cavities. Unlike other ducks, young stay in nests for up to two days before venturing out with their mothers. Female is very territorial and remains with the same mate for many years.

Greater Yellowlegs
Tringa melanoleuca

MIGRATION
WINTER

Size: 14" (36 cm)

Male: Tall bird with a bulbous head and long thin bill, slightly turned up. Gray streaking on chest. White belly. Long yellow legs.

Female: same as male

Juvenile: same as adult

Nest: ground; female builds; 1 brood per year

Eggs: 3-4; off-white with brown markings

Incubation: 22-23 days; female and male incubate

Fledging: 18-20 days; male and female feed young

Migration: complete, to Texas, Mexico, Central America and South America

Food: small fish, aquatic insects

Compare: Similar in size to breeding Willet (pg. 187), with a longer neck, smaller head and bright yellow legs. Greater Yellowlegs is an overall more brown bird than breeding Willet.

Stan's Notes: A common winter shorebird that can be identified by the slightly upturned bill and long yellow legs. Frequently seen resting on one leg. Its long legs carry it through deep water. Feeds by rushing forward through the water, plowing its bill or swinging it from side to side, catching small fish and insects. A skittish bird quick to give an alarm call, causing flocks to take flight. Quite often moves into the water prior to taking flight. Has a variety of "flight" notes that it gives when taking off. Nests on the ground near water on the northern tundra of Labrador and Newfoundland.

female

male pg. 19

Boat-tailed Grackle
Quiscalus major

YEAR-ROUND

Size: 14" (36 cm), female
16" (40 cm), male

Female: A golden brown chest and head with nearly black wings and tail, lacking iridescence.

Male: iridescent blue-black bird with a very long tail and bright yellow eyes

Juvenile: similar to female

Nest: cup; female builds; 2 broods per year

Eggs: 2-4; pale greenish blue, brown markings

Incubation: 13-15 days; female incubates

Fledging: 12-15 days; female feeds young

Migration: non-migrator; moves around to find food

Food: insects, berries, seeds, fish; visits feeders

Compare: Fairly distinctive. Not confused with many other birds. Found only along the coast.

Stan's Notes: A noisy bird of coastal saltwater and inland marshes, giving several harsh, high-pitched calls and several squeaks. Eats a wide variety of foods from grains to fish. Sometimes seen picking insects off the backs of cattle. Will also visit bird feeders. Makes a cup nest with mud or cow dung and grass. Nests in small colonies. Most nesting occurs in April and May. Boat-taileds on the Gulf coast have dark eyes, while Atlantic coast birds have bright yellow eyes.

male pg. 21

female

Great-tailed Grackle
Quiscalus mexicanus

YEAR-ROUND

Size: 15" (38 cm), female
18" (45 cm), male

Female: An overall brown bird with a gray-to-brown belly. Light brown-to-white eyes, eyebrows, throat and upper portion of chest.

Male: all-black bird with iridescent purple sheen on head and back, exceptionally long tail, bright yellow eyes

Juvenile: similar to female

Nest: cup; female builds; 1-2 broods per year

Eggs: 3-5; greenish blue with brown markings

Incubation: 12-14 days; female incubates

Fledging: 21-23 days; female feeds young

Migration: non-migrator to partial in Texas; will move around to find food

Food: insects, fruit, seeds; comes to seed feeders

Compare: Similar to the female Boat-tailed Grackle (pg. 183), which is found along the coast. Much larger than female Cowbird (pg. 141).

Stan's Notes: This is our largest grackle. It was once considered a subspecies of the Boat-tailed Grackle, which occurs along the Gulf coast. A bird that prefers to nest near water in an open habitat. A colony nester, males do not participate in nest building, incubation or raising of young. Males rarely fight, but females will squabble over nest sites and materials. Several females mate with one male. It is expanding northward, moving into northern states. Western populations tend to be larger than the eastern. Song varies from population to population.

breeding

winter pg. 301

displaying

Willet
Catoptrophorus semipalmatus

YEAR-ROUND
MIGRATION

Size: 15" (38 cm)

Male: Brown breeding plumage with a brown bill and legs. White belly. Distinctive black and white wing lining pattern, seen in flight or during display.

Female: same as male

Juvenile: similar to breeding adult, more tan in color

Nest: ground; female builds; 1 brood per year

Eggs: 3-5; olive green with dark markings

Incubation: 24-28 days; male and female incubate

Fledging: unknown days; female and male feed young

Migration: complete to non-migrator, to coastal Texas, Mexico, Central and South America

Food: aquatic insects

Compare: Slightly larger than the Greater Yellowlegs (pg. 181), which has a longer neck, smaller head and yellow legs. Greater Yellowlegs lacks the Willet's distinctive black and white wing linings.

Stan's Notes: Seen during migration throughout Texas and a year-round resident along the coast. Northern birds pass through coastal Texas to destinations farther south. It appears a rich, warm brown during breeding season and rather plain gray in winter, but always has a striking black and white wing pattern when seen during flight. Uses its black and white wing patches to display to its mate. Named after the "pill-will-willet" call it gives during the breeding season. Gives a "kip-kip-kip" alarm call when it takes flight. Nests in other western states and Canada.

winter male

male

female

Ruddy Duck
Oxyura jamaicensis

WINTER

Size: 15" (38 cm)

Male: Compact reddish brown body with a black crown and nape. Large bright white cheek patch. Distinctive light blue bill. Long tail, often raised above water. Winter has a dull brown-to-gray body and dark bill.

Female: similar to winter male, lacks the large white cheek patch and blue bill

Juvenile: similar to female

Nest: ground; female builds; 1 brood per year

Eggs: 6-8; pale white without markings

Incubation: 23-26 days; female incubates

Fledging: 42-48 days; female and male feed young

Migration: complete, to Texas

Food: aquatic insects and plants

Compare: The male Ring-necked Duck (pg. 65) has gray sides and a white ring around the bill. Look for a light blue bill and raised tail to help identify the male Ruddy Duck.

Stan's Notes: A diving duck with a unique appearance. Awkward on land. Often secretive, found on ponds and bays. Flushes quickly and stays away for a long time. Breeding male displays like a windup toy, ratcheting his head up and down, making muffled sounds and a staccato "pop." Male breeds with more than one female. Female lays some eggs in other duck nests. Male often seen with female and ducklings, but is not the father. Babies can dive soon after hatching. Has a blue bill, but is not the species that duck hunters call Blue Bill.

male

female

Green-winged Teal
Anas crecca

WINTER

Size: 15" (38 cm)

Male: A chestnut head with a dark green patch in back of eyes extending down to the nape of neck and outlined in white. Gray body with a butter yellow tail. Green speculum.

Female: light brown in color with black spots, green speculum, small black bill

Juvenile: same as female

Nest: ground; female builds; 1 brood per year

Eggs: 8-10; creamy white without markings

Incubation: 21-23 days; female incubates

Fledging: 32-34 days; female teaches young to feed

Migration: complete, to Texas

Food: aquatic plants and insects

Compare: Male Green-winged is not as colorful as the male Wood Duck (pg. 327). Female Green-winged is very similar to the larger female Cinnamon Teal (pg. 195), which lacks the dark line through eyes and has a larger bill. The female Blue-winged Teal (pg. 193) is similar in size and has a slight white mark at base of bill.

Stan's Notes: One of the smallest dabbling ducks, it tips forward in the water to feed off the bottom of shallow ponds. This behavior makes it vulnerable to ingesting spent lead shot, which can cause death. It walks well on land and also feeds in fields and woodlands. Known for its fast and agile flight, groups spin and wheel through the air in tight formation. Green speculum most obvious in flight.

Blue-winged Teal
Anas discors

YEAR-ROUND
SUMMER
WINTER

Size: 15-16" (38-40 cm)

Male: Small, plain-looking brown duck speckled with black. A gray head with a large white crescent-shaped mark at base of bill. Black tail with small white patch. Blue wing patch (speculum) usually seen only in flight.

Female: duller version of male, lacks facial crescent mark and white patch on tail, showing only slight white at base of bill

Juvenile: same as female

Nest: ground; female builds; 1 brood per year

Eggs: 8-11; creamy white

Incubation: 23-27 days; female incubates

Fledging: 35-44 days; female feeds young

Migration: complete, to Texas, Mexico and Central America, non-migrator in parts of Texas

Food: aquatic plants, seeds, aquatic insects

Compare: Male Blue-winged has a distinct white face marking. The female Blue-winged is smaller than the female Mallard (pg. 213). Female Green-winged Teal (pg. 191) is similar in size, but lacks white at base of bill.

Stan's Notes: One of the smallest ducks in North America. Nests some distance from water. Female performs a distraction display to protect nest and young. Male leaves female near end of incubation. Planting crops and cultivating to pond edges have caused a decline in population. Widespread nesting, breeding as far north as Alaska. One of the most common and longest distance migrating ducks.

Cinnamon Teal
Anas cyanoptera

MIGRATION
SUMMER
WINTER

Size: 16" (40 cm)

Male: Deep cinnamon head, neck and belly. Light brown back. Dark gray bill. Deep red eyes. Non-breeding (July to September) male is overall brown with a red tinge.

Female: overall brown with a pale brown head, long shovel-like bill, green patch on wings

Juvenile: similar to female

Nest: ground; female builds; 1 brood per year

Eggs: 7-12; pinkish white without markings

Incubation: 21-25 days; female incubates

Fledging: 40-50 days; female teaches young to feed

Migration: partial migrator to complete, to southern Texas, Mexico

Food: aquatic plants and insects, seeds

Compare: Male Teal shares the cinnamon sides of the larger male Northern Shoveler (pg. 333), but lacks Shoveler's green head and very large spoon-shaped bill. Female Cinnamon Teal looks very similar to the smaller female Green-winged Teal (pg. 191), which has a dark line through the eyes.

Stan's Notes: The male teal is one of the most stunningly beautiful ducks. When threatened, the female feigns a wing injury to lure predators away from young. Prefers to nest along alkaline marshes and shallow lakes, within 75 yards (68 m) of water. Mallards and other ducks often lay eggs in teal nests, resulting in many nests totaling over 15 eggs.

YEAR-ROUND

Barn Owl
Tyto alba

Size: 16" (40 cm); up to 3½-foot wingspan

Male: A "non-eared" owl with a rusty brown back of head, back, wings and tail. Heart-shaped white face, outlined in darker rusty brown. White chest and belly. Dark eyes. Long gray legs. Gray feet. Yellow bill.

Female: similar to male, often with a rusty wash over the chest and belly

Juvenile: light gray to white, fuzzy-looking overall

Nest: cavity, occasionally on a cliff crevice; female builds; 1 brood per year

Eggs: 3-7; white without markings

Incubation: 30-34 days; female incubates

Fledging: 52-56 days; male and female feed young

Migration: non-migrator

Food: small mammals, birds, snakes

Compare: Larger than the Burrowing Owl (pg. 163), which lacks the heart-shaped white face of the Barn Owl.

Stan's Notes: This owl is well known for nesting in old barns (hence the common name), but will also nest in any dark cavity on cliffs or in trees. Male feeds female during incubation. Clutch size depends on the availability of prey–the more prey, the larger the clutch. Young hatch one per day (asynchronously) over two weeks, creating a range of ages in the nest. Will sway back and forth with lowered head when confronted.

soaring

YEAR-ROUND

Red-shouldered Hawk
Buteo lineatus

Size: 14½-18½" (37-47 cm); up to 3½-ft. wingspan

Male: Reddish (cinnamon) head, shoulders, chest and belly. Wings and back are dark brown with white spots. Long tail with thin white bands and wide black bands. Obvious red wing linings, seen in flight.

Female: same as male

Juvenile: similar to adult, lacks the cinnamon color, has a white chest with dark spots

Nest: platform; female and male build; 1 brood per year

Eggs: 2-4; white with dark markings

Incubation: 27-29 days; female and male incubate

Fledging: 39-45 days; female and male feed young

Migration: non-migrator to partial migrator; winters in the U.S.

Food: reptiles, amphibians, large insects, birds

Compare: The Red-tailed (pg. 225) has a white chest. Cooper's Hawk (pg. 303) has a slimmer body and longer tail. Sharp-shinned Hawk (pg. 295) lacks the reddish head and belly.

Stan's Notes: A woodland hawk, seen in backyards. Prefers to hunt along edges of forests, spotting snakes, frogs, insects, an occasional small bird and other prey as it perches. Often seen flapping with an alternating gliding pattern. Very vocal hawk with a distinct scream. Mates when 2-3 years old. Stays in same territory for many years. Starts building nest in February. Young leave the nest by June.

male pg. 63

female

Lesser Scaup
Aythya affinis

Size: 16-17" (40-43 cm)

Female: Overall brown duck with dull white patch at base of light gray bill. Yellow eyes.

Male: white and gray, the chest and head appear nearly black but head appears purple with green highlights in direct sun, yellow eyes

Juvenile: same as female

Nest: ground; female builds; 1 brood per year

Eggs: 8-14; olive buff without markings

Incubation: 22-28 days; female incubates

Fledging: 45-50 days; female teaches young to feed

Migration: complete, to Texas, Mexico, Central America and northern South America

Food: aquatic plants and insects

Compare: Similar size as the female Ring-necked Duck (pg. 203), but lacking the white ring around the bill. Male Blue-winged Teal (pg. 193) is slightly smaller and has a crescent-shaped white mark at the base of bill. The female Wood Duck (pg. 209) is larger with white around the eyes.

Stan's Notes: A common diving duck. Often seen in large flocks on lakes, ponds and sewage lagoons. Completely submerges itself to feed on the bottom of lakes (unlike dabbling ducks, which only tip forward to reach the bottom). Note the bold white stripe under the wings when in flight. Has an interesting baby-sitting arrangement in which groups of young are tended by 1-3 adult females. A winter resident throughout Texas.

male pg. 65

female

Ring-necked Duck
Aythya collaris

WINTER

Size: 17" (43 cm)

Female: Mainly brown back with light brown sides, a gray face and dark brown crown. White eye-ring extends into a line behind eye. A white ring around a light blue bill. Top of head is peaked.

Male: black head, breast and back, sides are gray to nearly white, a bold white ring around a light blue bill and second ring at the base of bill, top of head is peaked

Juvenile: similar to female

Nest: ground; female builds; 1 brood per year

Eggs: 8-10; olive gray to brown without markings

Incubation: 26-27 days; female incubates

Fledging: 49-56 days; female teaches young to feed

Migration: complete, to Texas, Mexico, Central America

Food: aquatic plants and insects

Compare: Female Lesser Scaup (pg. 201) is similar in size. Look for female Ring-necked's white ring around the bill.

Stan's Notes: A common winter duck throughout Texas. A diving duck, watch for it to dive underwater to forage for food. Takes to flight by springing up off water. Was named "Ring-necked" because of the cinnamon collar (nearly impossible to see in the field). Also called Ring-billed Duck due to the white ring on its bill, and Blue Bill by duck hunters.

male pg. 67

female

Hooded Merganser
Lophodytes cucullatus

WINTER

Size: 16-19" (40-48 cm)

Female: Sleek brown and rust bird with a red head. Ragged "hair" on back of head. Long, thin brown bill.

Male: same size and shape as female, but a black back and rust sides, crest "hood" raises to reveal large white patch, long black bill

Juvenile: similar to female

Nest: cavity; female lines old woodpecker hole; 1 brood per year

Eggs: 10-12; white without markings

Incubation: 32-33 days; female incubates

Fledging: 71 days; female feeds young

Migration: complete, to the eastern half of Texas

Food: small fish, aquatic insects

Compare: Larger than female Lesser Scaup (pg. 201), which has a dull white patch at base of bill.

Stan's Notes: A small diving bird of shallow ponds, sloughs, lakes and rivers. Rarely found away from wooded areas, where it nests in natural cavities or nest boxes. The female will "dump" eggs into other female Hooded Merganser nests, resulting in 20-25 eggs in some nests. Known to share a nesting cavity with a Wood Duck, sitting side by side. Male Hooded Merganser can voluntarily raise and lower its crest to show off the white head patch.

Whimbrel

Numenius phaeopus

WINTER

Size: 18" (45 cm)

Male: Heavily streaked bird, light brown to gray. A long down-curved bill and multiple dark brown stripes on crown. Dark line through eyes. Legs are light gray to blue.

Female: same as male

Juvenile: similar to adult

Nest: ground; female and male construct; 1 brood per year

Eggs: 3-4; olive green with dark markings

Incubation: 27-28 days; male and female incubate

Fledging: 35-42 days; female and male feed young

Migration: complete, to coastal Texas, Mexico, Central and South America

Food: insects, snails, worms, leeches, berries

Compare: Breeding Willet (pg. 187) is smaller, lacks a crown with brown stripes and long down-curved bill. Greater Yellowlegs (pg. 181) is also smaller and has yellow legs.

Stan's Notes: A winter resident, easily identified by its very long down-curved bill and brown stripes on head. Uses its bill to probe deep into sand and mud for insects. Unlike the other shorebirds, berries become an important food source in summer. Is very vocal, giving single note whistles. Returns to tundra of northern Alaska to nest. Doesn't breed until age 3. Has a long-term pair bond. Adults leave breeding grounds up to two weeks before the young leave.

male pg. 327

female

Wood Duck

Aix sponsa

YEAR-ROUND
SUMMER
WINTER

Size: 17-20" (43-50 cm)

Female: A small brown dabbling duck. Bright white eye-ring and a not-so-obvious crest. A blue patch on wing is often hidden.

Male: highly ornamented with a green head and crest patterned with white and black, rusty chest, white belly and red eyes

Juvenile: same as female

Nest: cavity; female lines old woodpecker cavity; 1 brood per year

Eggs: 10-15; creamy white without markings

Incubation: 28-36 days; female incubates

Fledging: 56-68 days; female teaches young to feed

Migration: non-migrator to partial migrator in Texas

Food: aquatic insects, plants, seeds

Compare: Female Mallard (pg. 213) and female Blue-winged Teal (pg. 193) lack the bright white eye-ring and crest. The female Northern Shoveler (pg. 219) is larger and has a large spoon-shaped bill.

Stan's Notes: A common duck of quiet, shallow backwater ponds. Nests in old woodpecker holes or in nest boxes. Often seen flying deep in forests or perched high on tree branches. Female takes to flight with a loud squealing call, entering nest cavity from full flight. Will lay eggs in a neighboring female nest (egg dumping), resulting in some clutches in excess of 20 eggs. Young stay in nest cavity only 24 hours after hatching, then jump from up to 30 feet (9 m) to the ground or water to follow their mother, never returning to the nest.

male pg. 353

female

Redhead
Aythya americana

WINTER

Size: 19" (48 cm)

Female: Plain, soft brown duck with gray-to-white wing linings. Top of head is rounded. Two-toned bill, gray with a black tip.

Male: rich red head and neck with a black breast and tail, gray sides, smoky gray wings and back, tricolored bill with a light blue base, white ring and black tip

Juvenile: similar to female

Nest: cup; female builds; 1 brood per year

Eggs: 9-14; pale white without markings

Incubation: 24-28 days; female and male incubate

Fledging: 56-73 days; female shows the young what to eat

Migration: complete, to Texas

Food: seeds, aquatic plants, insects

Compare: The female Northern Shoveler (pg. 219) is a lighter brown with an exceptionally large shovel-shaped bill.

Stan's Notes: A duck of permanent large bodies of water. Forages along the shoreline, feeding on seeds, aquatic plants and insects. Usually builds nest directly on surface of water, using large mats of vegetation. Female lays up to 75 percent of its eggs in the nests of other Redheads and several other duck species. Nests primarily in the Prairie Pothole region of the northern Great Plains. The overall populations seem to be increasing at about 2-3 percent each year. Winters throughout Texas where it can find water.

male pg. 331

female

Mallard
Anas platyrhynchos

SUMMER
WINTER

Size: 19-21" (48-53 cm)

Female: All brown with orange and black bill. Small blue and white wing mark (speculum).

Male: large, bulbous green head, white necklace, rust brown or chestnut chest, combination of gray and white on the sides, yellow bill, orange legs and feet

Juvenile: same as female, but with a yellow bill

Nest: ground; female builds; 1 brood per year

Eggs: 7-10; greenish to whitish, unmarked

Incubation: 26-30 days; female incubates

Fledging: 42-52 days; female leads young to food

Migration: complete, to Texas

Food: seeds, plants, aquatic insects; will come to ground feeders offering corn

Compare: Female Gadwall (pg. 215) has a gray bill with orange sides. Female Northern Pintail (pg. 217) is similar to female Mallard, but it has a gray bill. Female Northern Shoveler (pg. 219) has a spoon-shaped bill. Female Wood Duck (pg. 209) has a white eye-ring.

Stan's Notes: A familiar duck of lakes and ponds, it's considered a type of dabbling duck, tipping forward in shallow water to feed on aquatic plants on the bottom. The name "Mallard" comes from the Latin *masculus*, meaning "male," referring to the habit of males not taking part in raising ducklings. Both female and male have white tails and white underwings. Black central tail feathers of male curl upward. Will return to place of birth.

male pg. 307

female

Gadwall
Anas strepera

YEAR-ROUND
WINTER

Size: 20" (50 cm)

Female: Very similar to the female Mallard. Mottled brown with pronounced color change from dark brown body to light brown neck and head. Wing linings are bright white, seen in flight. Small white wing patch, seen when swimming. Gray bill with orange sides.

Male: plump gray duck with a brown head and distinctive black rump, white belly, bright white wing linings, small white wing patch, chestnut-tinged wings, gray bill

Juvenile: similar to female

Nest: ground; female lines the nest with fine grass and down feathers plucked from her chest; 1 brood per year

Eggs: 8-11; white without markings

Incubation: 24-27 days; female incubates

Fledging: 48-56 days; young feed themselves

Migration: complete to non-migrator in Texas

Food: aquatic insects

Compare: The female Gadwall is very similar to female Mallard (pg. 213). Look for Gadwall's white wing patch and gray bill with orange sides.

Stan's Notes: A duck of shallow marshes. Consumes mostly plant material, dunking its head in water to feed rather than tipping forward, like other dabbling ducks. Walks well on land; feeds in fields and woodlands. Nests within 300 feet (100 m) of water. Often in pairs with other duck species. Establishes pair bond during winter.

Northern Pintail
Anas acuta

YEAR-ROUND
WINTER

Size: 20" (50 cm), female
25" (63 cm), male

Male: A slender, elegant duck with a brown head, white neck, gray body and extremely long, narrow black tail. Gray bill. Non-breeding has a pale brown head that lacks the clear demarcation between the brown head and white neck. Lacks long tail feathers.

Female: mottled brown body with a paler head and neck, long tail, gray bill

Juvenile: similar to female

Nest: ground; female builds; 1 brood per year

Eggs: 6-9; olive green without markings

Incubation: 22-25 days; female incubates

Fledging: 36-50 days; female teaches young to feed

Migration: complete, to Texas and Mexico

Food: aquatic plants and insects, seeds

Compare: The male Northern Pintail has a distinctive brown head and white neck. Look for the unique long tail feathers. The female Pintail is similar to female Mallard (pg. 213), but Mallard has an orange bill with black spots.

Stan's Notes: A common dabbling duck of marshes in the winter. Approximately 90 percent of its diet is aquatic plants from fresh water, except when the females feed heavily on aquatic insects prior to nesting, presumably to gain extra nutrients for egg production. Male holds tail upright from the water's surface. No other North American duck has such a long tail.

male pg. 333

female

Northern Shoveler
Anas clypeata

WINTER

Size: 20" (50 cm)

Female: Medium-sized brown duck speckled with black. Green speculum. An extraordinarily large spoon-shaped bill, almost always held pointed toward the water.

Male: iridescent green head, rusty sides and white breast, spoon-shaped bill

Juvenile: same as female

Nest: ground; female builds; 1 brood per year

Eggs: 9-12; olive without markings

Incubation: 22-25 days; female incubates

Fledging: 30-60 days; female leads young to food

Migration: complete, to Texas, Mexico, Central America

Food: aquatic insects, plants

Compare: Similar color as female Mallard (pg. 213), but Mallard lacks the Shoveler's large bill. Female Redhead (pg. 211) is overall lighter brown and has a dark gray bill with a black tip. Look for Shoveler's large spoon-shaped bill to help identify.

Stan's Notes: One of several species of shoveler, so called because of the peculiar shape of its bill. The Northern Shoveler is the only species of these ducks in North America. Found in small flocks of 5-10, swimming low in water with its large bill pointed toward the water, as if it's too heavy to lift. Feeds mainly by filtering tiny aquatic insects and plants from the water's surface with its bill. Winters in Texas where it can find water.

male pg. 305

female

soaring

Northern Harrier
Circus cyaneus

WINTER

Size: 20" (50 cm); up to 3½-foot wingspan

Female: A slim, low-flying hawk. Dark brown back with brown-streaked breast and belly. Large white rump patch and narrow black bands across tail. Tips of wings black. Yellow eyes.

Male: silver gray with large white rump patch and white belly, faint narrow bands across tail, tips of wings black, yellow eyes

Juvenile: similar to female, with an orange breast

Nest: platform, often on ground; female and male build; 1 brood per year

Eggs: 4-8; bluish white without markings

Incubation: 31-32 days; female incubates

Fledging: 30-35 days; male and female feed young

Migration: complete, to Texas, Mexico, Central America

Food: mice, snakes, insects, small birds

Compare: Slimmer than Red-tailed Hawk (pg. 225). Look for black tail bands, white rump patch and characteristic flight to help identify.

Stan's Notes: One of the easiest hawks to identify. Harriers glide just above ground, following contours of the land while searching for prey. Holds its wings just above the horizontal position, tilting back and forth in the wind, similar to Turkey Vultures. Formerly called Marsh Hawk due to its habit of hunting over marshes. Feeds on the ground. Will perch on the ground to preen and rest. At any age, has a distinctive owl-like face disk.

soaring

soaring juvenile

juvenile

YEAR-ROUND

Harris's Hawk
Parabuteo unicinctus

Size: 20" (50 cm); up to 3½-foot wingspan

Male: Overall dark brown hawk with rusty brown shoulders, wing linings and legs. Black tail with a bright white tip. Bright white rump. Yellow base of bill. Long yellow legs. Yellow feet. Rusty wing linings, seen in flight.

Female: same as male, but slightly larger

Juvenile: overall lighter brown with white streaks on breast, brown tail

Nest: platform; female and male build; 1-2 broods per year

Eggs: 3-4; pale white with some brown markings

Incubation: 33-36 days; female and male incubate

Fledging: 43-49 days; female and male feed young

Migration: non-migrator

Food: small mammals, snakes, birds, large insects

Compare: The Red-tailed Hawk (pg. 225) has a white breast. Look for rusty markings on wings, a white rump and white-tipped black tail.

Stan's Notes: Usually in semiarid woodlands near water. Common to see it in city parks and suburban yards. Unlike most raptors, it hunts in small groups, usually family members. Cooperative hunting is more successful than hunting singly and enables the capture of larger prey such as jackrabbits. Nest duties often shared between females and males and sometimes by other family members. Young hatch up to a couple days apart (asynchronous), leading to young developing at different times. Parents feed the young for up to six months. Produces a second brood in years with abundant food.

223

soaring

Western

soaring

Eastern

YEAR-ROUND

Red-tailed Hawk
Buteo jamaicensis

Size: 19-23" (48-58 cm); up to 4-foot wingspan

Male: Large hawk with amazing variety of colors from bird to bird, from chocolate brown to nearly all white. Usually a white breast and a distinctive brown belly band. Rust red tail, usually seen only from above. Underside of wing is white with a small dark patch on the leading edge near shoulder.

Female: same as male, only slightly larger

Juvenile: similar to adults, lacking the red tail, has a speckled chest and light eyes

Nest: platform; male and female build; 1 brood per year

Eggs: 2-3; white without markings or sometimes marked with brown

Incubation: 30-35 days; female and male incubate

Fledging: 45-46 days; male and female feed young

Migration: non-migrator to partial migrator

Food: mice, birds, snakes, insects, mammals

Compare: Red-shouldered Hawk (pg. 199) is much smaller and lacks a red tail and white chest.

Stan's Notes: A common hawk of open country and in cities in the state, frequently seen perching on freeway light posts, fences and trees. Look for it circling over open fields and roadsides, searching for prey. Their large stick nests are commonly seen in large trees along roads. Nests are lined with finer material such as evergreen tree needles. Will return to the same nest site each year. Develops red tail in the second year. Western variety has a brown chin, while Eastern has a white chin. Map reflects the combined range.

225

Barred Owl
Strix varia

YEAR-ROUND

Size: 20-24" (50-60 cm); up to 3½-foot wingspan

Male: A chunky brown and gray owl with a large head and dark brown eyes. Dark horizontal barring on upper chest. Vertical streaks on lower chest and belly. Yellow bill and feet.

Female: same as male, only slightly larger

Juvenile: light gray with a black face

Nest: cavity; does not add any nesting material; 1 brood per year

Eggs: 2-3; white without markings

Incubation: 28-33 days; female incubates

Fledging: 42-44 days; female and male feed young

Migration: non-migrator

Food: mammals, birds, fish, reptiles, amphibians

Compare: Lacks the "horns" of the Great Horned Owl (pg. 237) and ear tufts of the tiny Eastern Screech-Owl (pg. 283). Eastern Screech-Owl is less than half the size of Barred Owl.

Stan's Notes: A very common owl in eastern Texas that can often be seen hunting during the day, perching and watching for mice, birds and other prey. One of the few owls to take fish out of a lake. Prefers dense deciduous woodlands with sparse undergrowth. Can be attracted with a simple nest box with a large opening, attached to a tree. The young stay with parents for up to four months after fledging. Often sounds like a dog barking just before giving an eight-hoot call that sounds like, "Who-cooks-for-you? Who-cooks-for-you?" Great Horned Owl sounds like, "Hoo-hoo-hoo-hoooo!"

Plain Chachalaca
Ortalis vetula

YEAR-ROUND

Size: 21-23" (53-58 cm); up to 2-foot wingspan

Male: Varying shades of brown with a lighter buffy belly and undertail. A small head, long neck and small gray bill. Long, white-tipped dark tail often fans out during flight. Red patch of skin near throat during display.

Female: same as male, but lacks red skin near throat

Juvenile: similar to female

Nest: platform; female builds; 1 brood per year

Eggs: 2-3; cream to white without markings

Incubation: 22-27 days; female incubates

Fledging: 14-21 days; female and male feed young

Migration: non-migrator; moves around to find food

Food: seeds, fruit, insects, leaf buds; will come to ground feeders

Compare: Greater Roadrunner (pg. 231) is similar in size, but the Chachalaca is browner with a stockier body and a much smaller bill.

Stan's Notes: A large noisy bird, frequently seen walking on the ground, taking a dust bath or hopping from branch to branch in trees. Glides on short round wings from tree to tree in search of seeds and fruit. Expanded range due to increased backyard bird feeding. Nests in a tree 10-15 feet (3-4.5 m) above ground in a large nest built of large sticks. Young leave nest within hours to a couple days of hatching and follow parents to learn what to eat. Gathers in small groups in late summer and fall and moves to find food. Gives a loud "cha-cha-lac" followed by a group response, "cha-cha-la-ca," which can be heard repeatedly. Name comes from its familiar call.

Greater Roadrunner
Geococcyx californianus

YEAR-ROUND

Size: 23" (58 cm)

Male: Overall brown with white streaking. Has a conspicuous crest that can be raised and lowered. An extremely long tail and a long, pointed brown bill. Blue patch just behind eyes. Short round wings are darker brown than body. Long gray legs with large feet.

Female: same as male

Juvenile: similar to adult

Nest: platform, low in a tree, shrub or cactus; the female and male build; 1-2 broods per year

Eggs: 4-6; white without markings

Incubation: 18-20 days; male and female incubate

Fledging: 16-18 days; male and female feed young

Migration: non-migrator

Food: insects, reptiles, small mammals and birds

Compare: Plain Chachalaca (pg. 229) is similar in size, but has a stockier body, a much smaller bill and lacks a crest.

Stan's Notes: Ground dweller with a very long tail and prominent crest when raised. Cuckoo family member known to run quickly across the ground to catch prey. A formidable predator, able to run up to 15 miles (24 km) per hour. Flies short distances, usually in a low glide after a running takeoff. Raises its tail high, lowers it slowly. A slow, descending, low-pitched "coo-coo-coo-coo." Male does most incubating and feeding of young. Performs a distraction display to protect the nest. Young can catch prey four weeks after leaving the nest.

juvenile

cinnamon wing linings

Long-billed Curlew
Numenius americanus

YEAR-ROUND
MIGRATION
SUMMER

Size: 23" (58 cm), including bill

Male: Cinnamon brown with an extremely long, down-curved bill. Long bluish legs. Darker cinnamon wing linings.

Female: same as male, but with a longer bill

Juvenile: same as adults, but with a shorter bill

Nest: ground; female builds; 1 brood per year

Eggs: 5-7; olive green with brown markings

Incubation: 27-30 days; female and male incubate, the female during day, male at night

Fledging: 32-45 days; female and male feed young

Migration: complete to non-migrator, to coastal Texas, coastal Mexico, Central and South America

Food: insects, worms, crabs, eggs

Compare: Greater Yellowlegs (pg. 181) is smaller and lacks the extremely long bill of the Curlew.

Stan's Notes: The largest of shorebirds, with an appropriate name. The extremely long bill is greater than half the length of its body. Female has a longer bill than male. Juvenile has a short bill, which grows into a long bill during the first six months. Uses bill to probe deep into mud for insects and worms. Female incubates during the day, male during the night. Although a shorebird, it is often in grass fields away from the shore. Breeds in open valleys and flatlands. Will fly up to 6 miles (10 km) from nest site to find food. Does not nest in most of Texas, nesting in western states such as Utah, Idaho, Wyoming and Montana. Spends winters along the Gulf coast.

winter

breeding

White-faced Ibis
Plegadis chihi

YEAR-ROUND
MIGRATION

Size: 23" (58 cm)

Male: Appears brown with rusty red (chestnut) on upper body. Glossy brown with green sheen on lower body. Long, down-curved gray bill. White border on a light red face. Orange-red legs and feet. Deep red eyes. Winter has less chestnut and a pink mask and legs.

Female: same as male

Juvenile: similar to winter adult

Nest: platform, on ground, low in shrub or small tree; female and male build; 1 brood a year

Eggs: 2-4; blue or green with brown markings

Incubation: 21-23 days; female and male incubate

Fledging: 30-35 days; female and male feed young

Migration: complete to non-migrator, to coastal Texas, Mexico

Food: insects, crayfish, frogs, small fish, shellfish

Compare: American Avocet (pg. 71) is mostly black and white with an upturned bill.

Stan's Notes: Of the three ibis species in the U.S., this one is seen during migration throughout Texas and year-round along the Gulf coast. Usually found in marshes and estuaries. When near and in good light, appears glossy red with green, blue and purple highlights. Uses its long bill to find and eat aquatic insects and fish. Large groups fly in a straight line. Rapid, shallow wing beat, then a short glide. Nests close to the water in large colonies with egrets and herons. Builds a loose nest of thin twigs, leaves and roots, lined with green leaves. Common name comes from the white outline on face.

Great Horned Owl
Bubo virginianus

YEAR-ROUND

Size: 21-25" (53-63 cm); up to 3½-foot wingspan

Male: Robust brown "horned" owl. Bright yellow eyes and V-shaped white throat resembling a necklace. Horizontal barring on the chest.

Female: same as male, only slightly larger

Juvenile: similar to adults, lacking ear tufts

Nest: no nest; takes over nests of crows, Great Blue Herons and hawks, or will use partial cavities, stumps or broken-off trees; 1 brood per year

Eggs: 2; white without markings

Incubation: 26-30 days; female incubates

Fledging: 30-35 days; male and female feed young

Migration: non-migrator

Food: mammals, birds (ducks), snakes, insects

Compare: Barred Owl (pg. 227) has dark eyes and no "horns." Burrowing Owl (pg. 163) is much smaller, has long legs and lacks feather tuft "horns." Horned is over twice the size of its cousin, Eastern Screech-Owl (pg. 283).

Stan's Notes: One of the earliest nesting birds in the state, laying eggs in January and February. Has excellent hearing; able to hear a mouse moving beneath a foot of snow. "Ears" are actually tufts of feathers (horns) and have nothing to do with hearing. Not able to turn its head all the way around. Wing feathers are ragged on ends, resulting in a silent flight. The eyelids close from the top down, like humans. Fearless, it is one of the few animals that will kill skunks and porcupines. Because of this, it is sometimes called Flying Tiger.

soaring

juvenile

Golden Eagle
Aquila chrysaetos

YEAR-ROUND
WINTER

Size: 30-40" (76-102 cm); up to 7-foot wingspan

Male: Uniform dark brown with golden head and nape of neck. Yellow around the base of bill and yellow feet.

Female: same as male

Juvenile: similar to adult, but has white wrist patches and white base of tail

Nest: platform, on cliff; female and male build; 1 brood per year

Eggs: 2; white with brown markings

Incubation: 43-45 days; female and male incubate

Fledging: 66-75 days; female and male feed young

Migration: non-migrator to partial migrator; will move around to find food

Food: mammals, birds, reptiles, insects

Compare: Similar to adult Bald Eagle (pg. 81), but lacks the white head and tail. The juvenile Golden Eagle, a large dark bird with white markings, is often confused with juvenile Bald Eagle.

Stan's Notes: Large and powerful bird of prey that has no trouble taking larger prey such as jackrabbits. Hunts by perching or soaring and watching for movement. Inhabits mountainous terrain, requiring large territories to provide large supply of food. Thought to mate for life, renewing pair bond late in winter with spectacular high-flying courtship displays. Usually nests on cliff faces, rarely in trees. Uses well-established nest that has been used for generations. Not uncommon for it to add things to nest such as antlers, bones and barbed wire.

YEAR-ROUND

Wild Turkey
Meleagris gallopavo

Size: 36-48" (90-120 cm)

Male: Large, plump brown and bronze bird with striking blue and red bare head. Fan tail and long, straight black beard in center of chest. Spurs on legs.

Female: thinner and less striking than male, usually lacking breast beard

Juvenile: same as adult of the same sex

Nest: ground; female builds; 1 brood per year

Eggs: 10-12; buff white with dull brown markings

Incubation: 27-28 days; female incubates

Fledging: 6-10 days; female leads young to food

Migration: non-migrator

Food: insects, seeds, fruit

Compare: This bird is quite distinctive and unlikely to be confused with others.

Stan's Notes: The largest native game bird in Texas, and the bird from which the domestic turkey was bred. It almost became our national bird, losing to the Bald Eagle by a single vote. A strong flier that can approach 60 miles (97 km) per hour. Able to fly straight up, then away. Eyesight is three times better than human eyesight. Hearing is also excellent; can hear competing males up to a mile away. Males hold "harems" of up to 20 females. Males are toms, females are hens and young are poults. Roosts in trees at night.

juvenile

breeding

chick-feeding adult

Brown Pelican
Pelecanus occidentalis

YEAR-ROUND

Size: 48" (120 cm); up to 9-foot wingspan

Male: Gray brown body, black belly, exceptionally long gray bill. Breeding adult has white or yellow head with dark chestnut hind neck. Adult that is feeding chicks (chick-feeding adult) has a speckled white head. A non-breeding adult has a white head and neck.

Female: similar to male

Juvenile: brown with white breast and belly, does not acquire adult plumage until third year

Nest: platform; female and male build; 1 brood per year

Eggs: 2-4; white without markings

Incubation: 28-30 days; female and male incubate

Fledging: 71-86 days; female and male feed young

Migration: non-migrator

Food: fish

Compare: An unmistakable bird in Texas.

Stan's Notes: A coastal bird of Texas and recently an endangered species. Having suffered from eggshell thinning during the 1970s due to DDT and other pesticides, it is now reestablishing along the Gulf, East and West coasts. Captures fish by diving headfirst into the ocean, opening its large bill and "netting" fish with its gular pouch. Frequently seen sitting on posts around marinas. Nests in large colonies. Doesn't breed before the age of 3, when it obtains its breeding plumage.

Ruby-crowned Kinglet
Regulus calendula

WINTER

Size: 4" (10 cm)

Male: Small, teardrop-shaped green-to-gray bird with 2 white wing bars and a hidden ruby crown. White eye-ring.

Female: same as male, but lacking the ruby crown

Juvenile: same as female

Nest: pendulous; female builds; 1 brood per year

Eggs: 4-5; white with brown markings

Incubation: 11-12 days; female incubates

Fledging: 11-12 days; female and male feed young

Migration: complete, to Texas and Mexico

Food: insects, berries

Compare: The female American Goldfinch (pg. 379) is larger, but shares the same olive color and unmarked breast. Look for the white eye-ring of Ruby-crowned Kinglet.

Stan's Notes: One of the smaller birds in the state. It takes a quick eye to see the male's ruby crown. Most commonly seen during the spring and fall migrations, when groups travel together. Look for it flitting around thick shrubs low to the ground. Female builds an unusual pendulous (sac-like) nest, intricately woven and decorated on the outside with colored lichens and mosses stuck together with spider webs. The nest is suspended from a branch overlapped by leaves and usually is hung high in a mature tree. The common name "Kinglet" comes from the Anglo-Saxon word *cyning*, or "king," referring to the male's ruby crown, and the diminutive suffix "let," meaning "small." A winter resident throughout Texas.

WINTER

Red-breasted Nuthatch
Sitta canadensis

Size: 4½" (11 cm)

Male: A small gray-backed bird with a black cap and a prominent eye line. A rust red breast and belly.

Female: gray cap, pale undersides

Juvenile: same as female

Nest: cavity; female builds; 1 brood per year

Eggs: 5-6; white with red brown markings

Incubation: 11-12 days; female incubates

Fledging: 14-20 days; female and male feed young

Migration: irruptive; moves around the state in search of food

Food: insects, seeds; visits seed and suet feeders

Compare: Smaller than the White-breasted Nuthatch (pg. 255), with a red chest instead of white.

Stan's Notes: The Red-breasted Nuthatch behaves like the White-breasted Nuthatch, climbing down tree trunks headfirst. Similar to chickadees, visits seed feeders, quickly grabbing a seed and flying off to crack it open. Will wedge a seed into a crevice and pound it open with several sharp blows. The name "Nuthatch" comes from the Middle English moniker *nuthak*, referring to the bird's habit of wedging a seed into a crevice and hacking it open. Look for it in mature conifers, where it often extracts seeds from cones. Doesn't excavate a cavity as a chickadee might; rather, it takes over an old woodpecker or chickadee cavity. Common during some winters and absent in others.

male

female

juvenile

Verdin
Auriparus flaviceps

YEAR-ROUND

Size: 4½" (11 cm)

Male: Light gray to silvery overall. Lemon yellow head. Rusty red shoulder patch, frequently hidden. Short, pointed dark bill. Dark mark between bill and eyes. Dark legs and feet.

Female: duller than male

Juvenile: overall gray, lacks the yellow head, dark bill and rusty red shoulder patch

Nest: covered cup; male builds; 1-2 broods a year

Eggs: 4-5; bluish green with brown markings

Incubation: 8-10 days; female incubates

Fledging: 19-21 days; female and male feed young

Migration: non-migrator

Food: seeds, insects, fruit, nectar; comes to nectar feeders and orange halves

Compare: Smaller than the Tufted Titmouse (pg. 263), which has a crest and lacks a yellow head.

Stan's Notes: A very friendly bird that can be a regular visitor to nectar feeders and orange halves. Often hides its rusty red shoulder marks, confusing the novice bird watcher. Most easily identified as a tiny gray bird with a yellow head. Male builds several ball-shaped, conspicuous nests of thorny twigs, interweaves them with leaves and grass and lines them with feathers and plant down. Male shows the nest possibilities to female and she selects one. After fledging, young return to nest at night unlike most small birds, which leave and don't return for shelter. Often uses nest for several seasons.

Carolina Chickadee
Poecile carolinensis

YEAR-ROUND

Size: 5" (13 cm)

Male: Mostly gray bird with a black cap and chin. White face and chest with tan belly. Darker gray tail.

Female: same as male

Juvenile: same as adult

Nest: cavity; female and male build or excavate; 1-2 broods per year

Eggs: 5-7; white with reddish brown markings

Incubation: 11-12 days; female and male incubate

Fledging: 13-17 days; female and male feed young

Migration: non-migrator

Food: insects, seeds, fruit; comes to seed and suet feeders

Compare: Closely related to the Tufted Titmouse and Black-crested Titmouse (pg. 263), which have an erect crest and lack the Chickadee's black cap and chin.

Stan's Notes: One of the first birds to use a newly placed feeder. Flies to a feeder, grabs a single seed and carries it to a branch. To get to the meat inside, holds the seed down with feet and hammers the shell open with bill. Returns for another seed. A friendly bird that can be tamed and hand fed. Can be attracted with a nesting box that has a 1¼-inch entrance hole. Female will give a loud snake-like hiss when disturbed on the nest. Often seen with other birds (mixed flock) in winter. Song is a high, fast "chika-dee-dee-dee-dee."

female
pg. 121

male

pink-sided

Oregon male

Dark-eyed Junco
Junco hyemalis

WINTER

Size: 5½" (14 cm)

Male: A round, dark-eyed bird with slate gray-to-charcoal chest, head and back. White belly. Pink bill. Since the outermost tail feathers are white, tail appears as a white V in flight.

Female: same as male, only tan-to-brown color

Juvenile: similar to female, but has a streaked breast and head

Nest: cup; female and male construct; 2 broods per year

Eggs: 3-5; white with reddish brown markings

Incubation: 12-13 days; female incubates

Fledging: 10-13 days; male and female feed young

Migration: complete, to Texas

Food: seeds, insects; will come to seed feeders

Compare: Rarely confused with any other bird. Small flocks feed under bird feeders in winter.

Stan's Notes: Several junco species have now been combined into one, simply called Dark-eyed Junco (see lower insets). Spends the winter in the foothills and plains after snowmelt. Nests in a wide variety of wooded habitats in April and May. Adheres to a rigid social hierarchy, with dominant birds chasing less dominant birds. Look for its white outer tail feathers flashing while in flight. Most comfortable on the ground, juncos "double-scratch" with both feet to expose seeds and insects. Eats many weed seeds. Usually seen on the ground in small flocks. Doesn't nest in Texas.

White-breasted Nuthatch
Sitta carolinensis

YEAR-ROUND
WINTER

Size: 5-6" (13-15 cm)

Male: Slate gray with a white face and belly, and black cap and nape. Long thin bill, slightly upturned. Chestnut undertail.

Female: similar to male, gray cap and nape

Juvenile: similar to female

Nest: cavity; female and male construct; 1 brood per year

Eggs: 5-7; white with brown markings

Incubation: 11-12 days; female incubates

Fledging: 13-14 days; female and male feed young

Migration: non-migrator

Food: insects, seeds; visits seed and suet feeders

Compare: Red-breasted Nuthatch (pg. 247) is smaller with a rust red belly and a distinctive black eye line.

Stan's Notes: The nuthatch's habit of hopping headfirst down tree trunks helps it see insects and insect eggs that birds climbing up the trunk might miss. Incredible climbing agility comes from an extra-long hind toe claw or nail, nearly twice the size of the front toe claws. The name "Nuthatch" comes from the Middle English moniker *nuthak*, referring to the bird's habit of wedging a seed into a crevice and hacking it open. Often seen in flocks with chickadees and Downy Woodpeckers. Mated pairs will stay together all year, defending small territories. Listen for its characteristic spring call, "whi-whi-whi-whi," given from February to May. One of 17 worldwide nuthatch species.

male

first winter

female

Yellow-rumped Warbler
Dendroica coronata

YEAR-ROUND
WINTER

Size: 5-6" (13-15 cm)

Male: Slate gray bird with black streaks on breast. Yellow patches on rump, flanks and head. White chin and belly. Two white wing bars.

Female: duller than male, but same yellow patches

Juvenile: similar to female

Nest: cup; female builds; 2 broods per year

Eggs: 4-5; white with brown markings

Incubation: 12-13 days; female incubates

Fledging: 10-12 days; female and male feed young

Migration: partial migrator to non-migrator in Texas

Food: insects, berries; rarely comes to suet feeders

Compare: The male Wilson's Warbler (pg. 381) has a black cap. The male Common Yellowthroat (pg. 383) has a yellow chest and distinctive black mask. Look for patches of yellow on the rump, head, flanks and chin of Yellow-rumped Warbler to help identify.

Stan's Notes: A common warbler in Texas. Nests in coniferous and aspen forests. Flocks of hundreds are seen when northern birds join residents for the winter. Usually arrives in late September to early October. Frequently called Myrtle Warbler in eastern states and Audubon's Warbler in western states. Sometimes called Butter-butts due to the yellow patch on rump. Familiar call is a single, robust "chip," heard mostly in winter. Also has a wonderful song in spring.

breeding
pg. 131

winter

Least Sandpiper
Calidris minutilla

YEAR-ROUND
MIGRATION
WINTER

Size: 6" (15 cm)

Male: Overall gray to light brown winter plumage with a distinct brown breast band and light gray eyebrows. White belly and dull yellow legs. Short, down-curved black bill.

Female: same as male

Juvenile: similar to winter adult, but buff brown and lacking the breast band

Nest: ground; male and female construct; 1 brood per year

Eggs: 3-4; olive with dark markings

Incubation: 19-23 days; male and female incubate

Fledging: 25-28 days; male and female feed young

Migration: complete to non-migrator, to Texas, Mexico and Central America

Food: aquatic and terrestrial insects, seeds

Compare: The smallest of sandpipers. The yellow legs differentiate it from other tiny sandpipers, and the short, thin, down-curved bill helps to identify.

Stan's Notes: This is a tiny, tame sandpiper that can be approached without scaring. The smallest of peeps (sandpipers), it nests on the tundra in northern regions of Canada and Alaska. Prefers the grassy flats of saltwater and freshwater ponds. Its yellow legs can be hard to see in water, poor light or if covered with mud.

Black-throated Sparrow
Amphispiza bilineata

YEAR-ROUND

Size: 6" (15 cm)

Male: Overall smooth gray bird with bold black and white markings on head and face, and large black patch on the throat. Darker gray tail with white edges.

Female: same as male

Juvenile: similar to adult, lacks the black and white head pattern and black throat

Nest: cup; female builds; 1-2 broods per year

Eggs: 3-4; pale blue to white without markings

Incubation: 12-14 days; female incubates

Fledging: 10-12 days; female and male feed young

Migration: non-migrator in Texas

Food: insects, seeds, leaf buds

Compare: Breeding male Lark Bunting (pg. 37) is black with white wing patches. Female and non-breeding male Lark Buntings (pg. 133) have heavily streaked breasts. Look for the black throat patch to identify the Sparrow.

Stan's Notes: A sparrow of desert scrub and rocky uplands. Male often perches on prominent spots in its territory and sings a short, simple, tinkling song or a high, bell-like "tee-tee-tee." Often holds off breeding until rainfall produces enough food. Female constructs a cup nest of dried grass low in a cactus and lines it with finer plant materials. Although the young are fed a diet of insects, adults will eat new green shoots of trees, shrubs and grasses along with insects and seeds. Forms small flocks in the winter of up to 20 individuals, often with other sparrow species.

Black-crested
Titmouse

YEAR-ROUND

Tufted Titmouse
Baeolophus bicolor

Size: 6" (15 cm)

Male: Slate gray bird with a white chest and belly. Pointed crest. Flanks are washed in a rusty brown. Gray legs and dark eyes.

Female: same as male

Juvenile: same as adult

Nest: cavity; female lines old woodpecker hole; 2 broods per year

Eggs: 5-7; white with brown markings

Incubation: 13-14 days; female incubates

Fledging: 15-18 days; female and male feed young

Migration: non-migrator

Food: insects, seeds, fruit; will come to seed and suet feeders

Compare: Titmouse is slightly larger than the Carolina Chickadee (pg. 251) and has a crest. Similar size and color as White-breasted Nuthatch (pg. 255), which lacks a crest.

Stan's Notes: Common feeder bird that is attracted with black oil sunflower seeds. Well known for its quickly repeated "peter-peter-peter" call. Prefix "Tit" comes from a Scandinavian word meaning "little." Suffix "mouse" is derived from the Old English word *mase*, meaning "bird." Simply translated, it is a "small bird." Notorious for pulling hair from sleeping dogs, cats and squirrels to line their nests. Attracted with nest boxes. Usually seen only 1-2 at a time. Male feeds female during courtship and nesting. The Black-crested Titmouse (see inset) occurs in central and southern parts of the state. Map reflects the combined range. Hybridization results in birds with dark gray crests and pale foreheads.

263

male pg. 347

female

SUMMER
WINTER

Vermilion Flycatcher
Pyrocephalus rubinus

Size: 6" (15 cm)

Female: A mostly gray bird with a gray head, neck and back. Nearly white chin and chest. Pink belly to undertail. Black tail. Thin black bill.

Male: crimson red head, crest, chin, breast and belly, black nape of neck, back, wings and tail, black line through eyes, thin black bill

Juvenile: similar to female, lacks a pink undertail

Nest: cup; female builds; 1-2 broods per year

Eggs: 2-4; white with brown markings

Incubation: 14-16 days; female and male incubate

Fledging: 14-16 days; female and male feed young

Migration: complete, to Mexico

Food: insects (mainly bees)

Compare: Similar body and bill shape as the phoebes of Texas and shares a similar habitat. Black Phoebe (pg. 43) is black with a white belly.

Stan's Notes: A summer resident with few staying all winter in extreme southern Texas. Often in open areas with shrubs and small trees close to water. Will perch on a thin branch, pumping tail up and down while waiting for an aerial insect. Flies out to snatch it, then returns to perch. Drops to the ground for terrestrial insects. Male raises its crest, fluffs chest feathers, fans tail and sings a song during a fluttery flight to court females. Female builds a shallow nest of twigs and grasses and lines it with downy plant material. Male feeds female during incubation and brooding.

YEAR-ROUND
SUMMER
WINTER

Eastern Phoebe
Sayornis phoebe

Size: 6½" (16 cm)

Male: Gray bird with dark wings, light olive green belly and a thin dark bill.

Female: same as male

Juvenile: same as adult

Nest: cup; female builds; 2 broods per year

Eggs: 4-5; white without markings

Incubation: 15-16 days; female incubates

Fledging: 15-16 days; male and female feed young

Migration: complete, to southern Texas and Mexico, non-migrator in eastern parts of Texas

Food: insects

Compare: Like most other olive gray birds, it is hard to distinguish identifying markings. Eastern Phoebe lacks any white eye-ring. Easier to identify by well-enunciated song, "fee-bee," or characteristic of hawking for insects.

Stan's Notes: A sparrow-sized bird often seen on the end of a dead branch. It sits in wait for a passing insect, flies out to catch it, then returns to the same branch, a process called hawking. Has a habit of pumping its tail up and down and spreading it when perched. Will build its nest under the eaves of a house, under a bridge or in culverts. Nest is constructed with mud, grass and moss, and lined with hair (and sometimes feathers). The name is derived from its characteristic song, "fee-bee," which is repeated over and over from the tops of dead branches.

YEAR-ROUND

Common Ground-Dove
Columbina passerina

Size: 6½" (16 cm)

Male: A very small dove with a short tail and a unique scalloped appearance on head and chest. Black-tipped reddish orange bill and slate gray crown. Pinkish gray underside. Bright chestnut wing linings, seen in flight.

Female: similar to male, but grayer and has a more uniform color

Juvenile: similar to adult

Nest: ground; female and male build; 2-4 broods per year

Eggs: 2-4; white without markings

Incubation: 12-14 days; female and male incubate

Fledging: 10-11 days; female and male feed young

Migration: non-migrator

Food: seeds, berries; will come to seed feeders

Compare: The Mourning Dove (pg. 175) is twice the size of Common Ground-Dove, lacks the scalloped appearance and chestnut-colored wing linings.

Stan's Notes: The smallest dove in Texas, formerly called Eastern Ground Dove. Known to continually bob its head. Frequently seen in pairs. Unafraid of humans and spends most of its time on the ground. While it usually nests on the ground, it sometimes builds a flimsy nest in a shrub or takes an abandoned nest low in a tree. Seen in open dry woodlands, old fields and pastures. Walks around with mechanical movements, bobbing its head and shuffling its feet like a wind-up toy.

YEAR-ROUND

Inca Dove
Columbina inca

Size: 8" (20 cm)

Male: A small thin-bodied dove, pale gray overall with a scalloped or scaly appearance due to dark-edged feathers. Lighter gray head with a dark thin bill and dark red eyes. Long thin tail. White outer tail feathers and dark rusty wing linings, seen in flight.

Female: same as male

Juvenile: similar to adult, lacks a scaly pattern

Nest: platform; female and male build; 2-3 broods per year

Eggs: 2; white without markings

Incubation: 12-14 days; female and male incubate

Fledging: 14-16 days; female and male feed young

Migration: non-migrator

Food: seeds, fruit; visits seed feeders on ground

Compare: One of the smallest doves in Texas. Scaly appearance assures correct identification.

Stan's Notes: Seen in many habitats including cities and suburbs, mostly in arid areas with some low scrubby growth. Male bows to female with tail fanned to show white sides. Outer wing feathers produce a buzzing sound in flight. Groups of up to 50 birds gather in summer and winter to find food. Roosts in large groups, sitting side by side or sometimes one on another. Huddles in "pyramids," sometimes stacked two or three individuals high. Constructs a loose platform nest of twigs, grass and leaves. Nest is sometimes built on the ground, low in a tree or shrub or in a hanging flower basket. Will also reuse the nest of larger doves such as Mourning Doves.

breeding
pg. 151

winter

Sanderling
Calidris alba

YEAR-ROUND
MIGRATION

Size: 8" (20 cm)

Male: The lightest sandpiper on the beach during winter. Winter plumage head and back are gray and belly is white. Black legs and bill. White wing stripe, seen only in flight.

Female: same as male

Juvenile: spotty black on the head and back, a white belly, black legs and bill

Nest: ground; male builds; 1-2 broods per year

Eggs: 3-4; greenish olive with brown markings

Incubation: 24-30 days; male and female incubate

Fledging: 16-17 days; female and male feed young

Migration: complete to non-migrator, to coastal Texas, Mexico, Central and South America

Food: insects

Compare: Same size as the winter plumage Spotted Sandpiper (pg. 149). Similar color as the winter Black-bellied Plover (pg. 293), but much smaller with a smaller bill.

Stan's Notes: One of the most common shorebirds in Texas, but mostly seen in gray winter plumage from August to April. Can be seen in groups on sandy beaches, running out with each retreating wave to feed. Look for a flash of white on wings when it is in flight. Occasionally the female will mate with several males (polyandry), resulting in males and the female incubating separate nests. Both sexes will perform a distraction display if threatened. Nests on the Arctic tundra. Rests by standing on one leg, tucking the other leg into its belly feathers. Will often hop away on one leg, moving away from pedestrians on the beach.

Eastern Kingbird
Tyrannus tyrannus

MIGRATION
SUMMER

Size: 8" (20 cm)

Male: Mostly black gray bird with white belly and chin. Black head and tail with a distinctive white band across the end of the tail. Has a concealed red crown that is rarely seen.

Female: same as male

Juvenile: same as adult

Nest: cup; male and female build; 1 brood a year

Eggs: 3-4; white with brown markings

Incubation: 16-18 days; female incubates

Fledging: 16-18 days; female and male feed young

Migration: complete, to Mexico, Central America and South America

Food: insects, fruit

Compare: Medium-sized bird, smaller than the Robin (pg. 285). Lacks any yellow of the Western Kingbird (pg. 403). The Eastern Phoebe (pg. 267) is smaller and lacks a white belly. Look for the white band at the end of Eastern Kingbird's tail to identify.

Stan's Notes: Found in open fields and prairies. Up to 20 birds migrate in a group. Returns to the mating ground in spring, where male and female defend territory. Acting unafraid of other birds and chasing the larger ones, it is perceived as having an attitude. Its bold behavior gave rise to the common name, King. Perches on tall branches and watches for insects. After flying out to catch them, returns to same perch (hawking). Very vocal in late summer, when entire families call back and forth while hunting for insects.

Gray Catbird
Dumetella carolinensis

YEAR-ROUND
MIGRATION
SUMMER

Size: 9" (22.5 cm)

Male: Handsome slate gray bird with black crown and a long, thin black bill. Often seen with its tail lifted up, exposing a chestnut patch under the tail.

Female: same as male

Juvenile: same as adult

Nest: cup; female and male construct; 2 broods per year

Eggs: 4-6; blue green without markings

Incubation: 12-13 days; female incubates

Fledging: 10-11 days; female and male feed young

Migration: complete to non-migrator, to eastern Texas

Food: insects, fruit

Compare: Larger than Eastern Phoebe (pg. 267), it lacks the Phoebe's olive belly. Similar size as Eastern Kingbird (pg. 275), but it lacks the Kingbird's white belly and white tail band.

Stan's Notes: A secretive bird that the Chippewa Indians named Bird That Cries With Grief due to its raspy call. The call sounds like the mewing of a house cat, hence the common name. Frequently mimics other birds, rarely repeating the same phrases. More often heard than seen. Nests in thick shrubs and quickly flies back into shrubs if approached. If a cowbird introduces an egg into a catbird nest, the catbird will quickly break it, then eject it.

YEAR-ROUND

Pyrrhuloxia
Cardinalis sinuatus

Size: 9" (22.5 cm)

Male: Overall gray with a bright red-tipped crest, red mask, throat, breast, belly and edges of wings and tail. Stout yellow bill. Dark eyes.

Female: similar to male, lacking red on face, throat, breast and belly, bill is gray to dull yellow

Juvenile: similar to female, has a dark gray bill, lacks red highlights

Nest: cup; female builds; 1 brood per year

Eggs: 2-4; gray to green with brown markings

Incubation: 12-14 days; female and male incubate

Fledging: 8-10 days; female and male feed young

Migration: non-migrator

Food: seeds, fruit, insects; will visit water elements and ground feeders

Compare: Female Northern Cardinal (pg. 159) has a black mask and a pointed red bill. Look for the Pyrrhuloxia's tall crest and long tail.

Stan's Notes: This is a secretive bird of arid brush, thorn scrub and mesquite habitat. Like its cousin, the Northern Cardinal, it is most active in early morning and just before sunset. Has a similar loud, crisp song like the cardinal and a single metallic "chip" call. Small flocks move around in the winter to find food. Feeds mostly on the ground, eating grass seeds and insects. Male feeds female during courtship and incubation. Female constructs a nest with twigs and grass in dense shrubs or thickets and lines it with fine grasses and plant fibers. Both defend home territory during the breeding season. Use water elements and ground feeders to attract it to your yard.

YEAR-ROUND

Loggerhead Shrike
Lanius ludovicianus

Size: 9" (22.5 cm)

Male: A gray head and back with black wings and mask across the eyes. A white chin, breast and belly. Black tail, legs and feet. Black bill with hooked tip. White wing patches, seen in flight.

Female: same as male

Juvenile: dull version of adult

Nest: cup; male and female construct; 1-2 broods per year

Eggs: 4-7; off-white with dark markings

Incubation: 16-17 days; female incubates

Fledging: 17-21 days; female and male feed young

Migration: non-migrator in Texas

Food: insects, lizards, small mammals, frogs

Compare: The Northern Mockingbird (pg. 287) has a similar color pattern, but lacks the black mask. Shrike is stockier than Mockingbird and perches in more open places. Cedar Waxwing (pg. 143) has a black mask, but is brown, not gray and black like Shrike.

Stan's Notes: The Loggerhead is a songbird that acts like a bird of prey. Known for skewering prey on barbed wire fences, thorns and other sharp objects to store or hold still while tearing apart to eat, hence its other common name, Butcher Bird. Feet are too weak to hold the prey it eats. Breeding bird surveys indicate declining populations in the Great Plains due to pesticides killing its major food source–grasshoppers.

red morph

gray morph

YEAR-ROUND

Eastern Screech-Owl
Megascops asio

Size: 9" (22.5 cm); up to 20-inch wingspan

Male: Small "eared" owl that occurs in one of two permanent color morphs. Is either mottled with gray and white or is red brown (rust) with white. Bright yellow eyes.

Female: same as male

Juvenile: lighter color than adult of the same morph, usually no ear tufts

Nest: cavity, former woodpecker cavity; does not add any nesting material; 1 brood per year

Eggs: 4-5; white without markings

Incubation: 25-26 days; female incubates, male feeds female during incubation

Fledging: 26-27 days; male and female feed young

Migration: non-migrator

Food: large insects, small mammals, birds, snakes

Compare: Burrowing Owl (pg. 163) is slightly larger and lacks ear tufts. Eastern Screech-Owl is hard to confuse with its considerably larger cousin, the Great Horned Owl (pg. 237).

Stan's Notes: A common owl active at dusk and during the night. Excellent hearing and eyesight. Will seldom give a screeching call; more commonly gives a tremulous, descending whiny trill, like a sound effect of a scary movie. Will nest in a wooden nest box. Often seen sunning themselves at nest box holes during the winter. Male and female may roost together at night, and are thought to mate for life. Different colorations are known as morphs. The gray morph is more common than the red.

**YEAR-ROUND
WINTER**

American Robin
Turdus migratorius

Size: 9-11" (22.5-28 cm)

Male: A familiar gray bird with a rusty red breast, and nearly black head and tail. White chin with black streaks. White eye-ring.

Female: similar to male, but with a gray head and a duller breast

Juvenile: similar to female, but has a speckled breast and brown back

Nest: cup; female builds with help from the male; 2-3 broods per year

Eggs: 4-7; pale blue without markings

Incubation: 12-14 days; female incubates

Fledging: 14-16 days; female and male feed young

Migration: non-migrator to complete in Texas

Food: insects, fruit, berries, worms

Compare: Familiar bird to all.

Stan's Notes: The robin is a complete migrator in northern states, but in Texas it is only a complete migrator in half of the state and a year-round resident the other. Northern birds join resident birds in the state during winter, increasing the population. Can be heard singing all night long during spring. Most people don't realize how easy it is to differentiate between male and female robins. Compare the male's dark, nearly black head and brick red breast with the female's gray head and dull red breast. Robins are not listening for worms when they cock their heads to one side. They are looking with eyes placed far back on the sides of their heads. This is a very territorial bird, often seen fighting its own reflection in windows.

displaying

Northern Mockingbird
Mimus polyglottos

YEAR-ROUND

Size: 10" (25 cm)

Male: Silvery gray head and back with light gray chest and belly. White wing patches, seen in flight or during display. Tail mostly black with white outer tail feathers. Black bill.

Female: same as male

Juvenile: dull gray, a heavily streaked chest, gray bill

Nest: cup; female and male build; 2 broods per year, sometimes more

Eggs: 3-5; blue green with brown markings

Incubation: 12-13 days; female incubates

Fledging: 11-13 days; female and male feed young

Migration: non-migrator in Texas

Food: insects, fruit

Compare: Loggerhead Shrike (pg. 281) has a similar color pattern, but is stockier, has a black mask and perches in more open places. Look for Mockingbird to spread its wings, flash its white wing patches and wag its tail from side to side.

Stan's Notes: Very animated. Performs an elaborate mating dance. Facing each other with heads and tails erect, pairs run toward each other, flashing white wing patches, and then retreat to cover nearby. Thought to flash wing patches to scare up insects when hunting. Sits for long periods of time on top of a shrub. Imitates other birds (vocal mimicry), hence the common name. Young males often sing at night. Often unafraid of people, allowing for close observation.

Curve-billed Thrasher
Toxostoma curvirostre

YEAR-ROUND

Size: 11" (28 cm)

Male: Large-bodied bird with a long tail and long downward-curved bill. Overall gray to light brown with faint spots on breast and belly. Eyes are dark yellow to orange.

Female: same as male

Juvenile: similar to adult, with a shorter bill

Nest: cup; female and male construct; 1-2 broods per year

Eggs: 3-4; pale blue green with brown markings

Incubation: 12-14 days; female and male incubate

Fledging: 14-18 days; female and male feed young

Migration: non-migrator

Food: insects, fruit, seeds; comes to seed feeders on the ground and water elements

Compare: Brown Thrasher (pg. 167) is rusty red with dark spots on the chest. Larger than Cactus Wren (pg. 153), which has a spotty dark patch on the chest and chestnut brown cap.

Stan's Notes: A familiar backyard bird that prefers scrubby desert habitat with mesquite, cactus and cholla. Will drive out any Cactus Wrens in its territory. Calls a loud, two-syllable "whit-wee." Feeds on the ground. Male follows female during courtship, singing a soft song. Builds nest in a spiny shrub or cactus, using twigs and grass and lining it with finer plant material. Will often reuse the nest after making minor repairs. Pairs often remain together all year. Young hatch on sequential days, requiring the parents to brood young for over two weeks. In hot weather parents shade the young from sun.

YEAR-ROUND
SUMMER

White-winged Dove
Zenaida asiatica

Size: 11" (28 cm)

Male: Light gray-to-brown dove. A conspicuous white edge on the wings. Small black dash underneath the cheeks. Vivid blue eye-rings around bright red eyes. Black wing tips with a white patch across the middle of wings, as seen in flight.

Female: same as male

Juvenile: similar to adult

Nest: platform; female and male build; 2-3 broods per year

Eggs: 2-4; white without markings

Incubation: 13-14 days; female and male incubate

Fledging: 13-16 days; female and male feed young

Migration: partial migrator to non-migrator

Food: seeds, fruit; will come to seed feeders

Compare: Slightly smaller than the Mourning Dove (pg. 175), which lacks the white line on closed wings and a white and black pattern in flight.

Stan's Notes: Very similar to the Mourning Dove in behavior and appearance. Feeds on the ground, pecking at seeds and tiny grains of rock to aid digestion. Parents feed young a regurgitated liquid called crop-milk the first few days of life. Male uses its white and black wing coloration to display to mate. May nest alone or in large colonies. This non-native species was introduced during the 1950s when captive birds were released in Florida. Gives a distinctive call, "coo-cuk-ca-roo."

breeding
pg. 57

winter

Black-bellied Plover
Pluvialis squatarola

YEAR-ROUND
MIGRATION

Size: 11-12" (28-30 cm)

Male: Winter plumage is uniform light gray with dark, nearly black streaks. White belly and chest. Faint white eyebrow mark. Black legs and bill.

Female: less black on belly and breast than male

Juvenile: grayer than adults, with much less black

Nest: ground; male and female construct; 1 brood per year

Eggs: 3-4; pinkish or greenish with black-brown markings

Incubation: 26-27 days; male and female incubate, the male during day, female at night

Fledging: 35-45 days; male feeds young, young learn quickly to feed themselves

Migration: complete to non-migrator, to coastal Texas, Mexico, Central and South America

Food: insects

Compare: Winter Spotted Sandpiper (pg. 149) has a shorter, thicker bill. The winter Sanderling (pg. 273) is smaller and has a smaller bill.

Stan's Notes: Males perform a "butterfly" courtship flight to attract females. Female leaves male and young about 12 days after the eggs hatch. Breeds at age 3. A common year-round resident along the coast. Begins arriving in July and August (fall migration) and leaves in April. During flight, in any plumage, displays a white rump and stripe on wings with black axillaries (armpits). Often darts across the ground to grab an insect and run.

soaring

juvenile

Sharp-shinned Hawk
Accipiter striatus

MIGRATION
WINTER

Size: 10-14" (25-36 cm); up to 2-foot wingspan

Male: Small woodland hawk with a gray back and head and a rusty red breast. Long tail with several dark tail bands, widest band at end of squared-off tail. Red eyes.

Female: same as male, only larger

Juvenile: same size as adults, with a brown back and heavily streaked breast, yellow eyes

Nest: platform; female builds; 1 brood per year

Eggs: 4-5; white with brown markings

Incubation: 32-35 days; female incubates

Fledging: 24-27 days; female and male feed young

Migration: complete, to Texas

Food: birds, small mammals

Compare: Nearly identical to Cooper's Hawk (pg. 303), only smaller. Look for the Sharp-shinned's squared tail compared with the rounded tail of the Cooper's. The Red-shouldered Hawk (pg. 199) has a reddish head and belly.

Stan's Notes: A common hawk of backyards and woodlands, often seen swooping in on birds visiting feeders. Its short rounded wings and long tail allow this hawk to navigate through thick stands of trees in pursuit of prey. Common name comes from the sharp keel on the leading edge of its "shin," though it is actually below rather than above the bird's ankle on the tarsus bone of foot. The tarsus in most birds is round. In flight, head doesn't protrude as far as the head of the Cooper's Hawk.

YEAR-ROUND

Eurasian Collared-Dove
Streptopelia decaocto

Size: 12½" (32 cm)

Male: Head, neck, chest and belly are pale gray to light tan. Slightly darker back, wings and tail. Black collar is bordered with white and extends around nape. Long squared-off tail.

Female: same as male

Juvenile: similar to adult

Nest: platform; female and male construct; 2-3 broods per year

Eggs: 3-5; creamy white without markings

Incubation: 12-14 days; female and male incubate

Fledging: 12-14 days; female and male feed young

Migration: non-migrator

Food: seeds

Compare: Slightly larger and lighter in color than the Mourning Dove (pg. 175). Look for a black collar and squared tail to help identify.

Stan's Notes: This non-native dove has spread into Texas, having moved into Florida in the 1980s after being introduced to the Bahamas. Reaching the northern states beginning in the late 1990s, it is expanding throughout North America. Predicted to spread throughout North America in the same way it spread throughout Europe from the Middle East. Nearly identical to a common pet bird species, the Ringed Turtle-Dove.

Rock Pigeon
Columba livia

YEAR-ROUND

Size: 13" (33 cm)

Male: No set color pattern. Gray to white, patches of iridescent greens and blues, usually with a light rump patch.

Female: same as male

Juvenile: same as adult

Nest: platform; female builds; 3-4 broods a year

Eggs: 1-2; white without markings

Incubation: 18-20 days; female and male incubate

Fledging: 25-26 days; female and male feed young

Migration: non-migrator

Food: seeds

Compare: Mourning Dove (pg. 175) is smaller, light brown and lacks all the color variations of Rock Pigeon. The Eurasian Collared-Dove (pg. 297) is gray with a black collar.

Stan's Notes: Also known as Domestic Pigeon, formerly known as Rock Dove. Introduced to North America from Europe by the early settlers. This bird is most common around cities and barnyards, where it scratches for seeds. One of the few birds that has a wide variety of colors, produced by years of selective breeding while in captivity. Parents feed their young a regurgitated liquid known as crop-milk for the first few days of life. One of the few birds that can drink without tilting its head back. Nests under bridges and on buildings, balconies, barns and sheds. Was once poisoned as a "nuisance city bird." Many cities now have Peregrine Falcons (not shown) that feed on Rock Pigeons, keeping their numbers in check.

breeding
pg. 187

displaying

winter

Willet
Catoptrophorus semipalmatus

YEAR-ROUND
MIGRATION

Size: 15" (38 cm)

Male: Winter plumage is gray with a gray bill and legs. White belly. A distinctive black and white wing lining pattern, seen in flight or during display.

Female: same as male

Juvenile: similar to breeding adult, more tan in color

Nest: ground; female builds; 1 brood per year

Eggs: 3-5; olive green with dark markings

Incubation: 24-28 days; male and female incubate

Fledging: unknown days; female and male feed young

Migration: complete to non-migrator, to coastal Texas, Mexico, Central and South America

Food: aquatic insects

Compare: Slightly larger than the Greater Yellowlegs (pg. 181), which has a longer neck, smaller head and yellow legs. Greater Yellowlegs lacks Willet's distinctive black and white wing linings.

Stan's Notes: Seen during migration throughout Texas and a year-round resident along the coast. Northern birds pass through coastal Texas to destinations farther south. It appears a rich, warm brown during breeding season and rather plain gray in winter, but always has a striking black and white wing pattern when seen during flight. Uses its black and white wing patches to display to its mate. Named after the "pill-will-willet" call it gives during the breeding season. Gives a "kip-kip-kip" alarm call when it takes flight. Nests in other western states and Canada.

soaring

juvenile

Cooper's Hawk
Accipiter cooperii

YEAR-ROUND
MIGRATION

Size: 14-20" (36-50 cm); up to 2½-foot wingspan

Male: Medium-sized hawk with short wings and long rounded tail with several black bands. Rusty breast and dark wing tips. Slate gray back. Bright yellow spot at base of gray bill (cere). Dark red eyes.

Female: similar to male, only slightly larger

Juvenile: brown back with brown streaks on breast, bright yellow eyes

Nest: platform; male and female build; 1 brood per year

Eggs: 2-4; greenish with brown markings

Incubation: 32-36 days; female and male incubate

Fledging: 28-32 days; male and female feed young

Migration: non-migrator to partial migrator; will move around to find food

Food: small birds, mammals

Compare: Nearly identical to the Sharp-shinned Hawk (pg. 295), only larger, darker gray and with a rounded-off tail. Slimmer body and longer tail than Red-shouldered Hawk (pg. 199).

Stan's Notes: Common woodland hawk. In flight, look for its large head, short wings and long tail. The stubby wings help it maneuver between trees while pursuing small birds. This hawk will come to feeders, hunting for unaware birds. Flies with long glides followed by a few quick flaps. Known to ambush prey, it will fly into heavy brush or even run on the ground in pursuit. Nestlings have gray eyes that become bright yellow at 1 year of age and dark red later.

female pg. 221

male

soaring

Northern Harrier
Circus cyaneus

WINTER

Size: 20" (50 cm); up to 3½-foot wingspan

Male: A slim, low-flying hawk. Silver gray with a large white rump patch and a white belly. Faint narrow bands across the tail. Tips of wings black. Yellow eyes.

Female: dark brown back, a brown-streaked breast and belly, large white rump patch, narrow black bands across tail and black wing tips, yellow eyes

Juvenile: similar to female, with an orange breast

Nest: platform, often on ground; female and male build; 1 brood per year

Eggs: 4-8; bluish white without markings

Incubation: 31-32 days; female incubates

Fledging: 30-35 days; male and female feed young

Migration: complete, to Texas, Mexico, Central America

Food: mice, snakes, insects, small birds

Compare: Slimmer than Red-tailed Hawk (pg. 225). Look for black tail bands, white rump patch and characteristic flight to help identify.

Stan's Notes: One of the easiest hawks to identify. Harriers glide just above ground, following contours of the land while searching for prey. Holds its wings just above the horizontal position, tilting back and forth in the wind, similar to Turkey Vultures. Formerly called Marsh Hawk due to its habit of hunting over marshes. Feeds on the ground. Will perch on the ground to preen and rest. At any age, has a distinctive owl-like face disk.

female pg. 215

male

Gadwall
Anas strepera

YEAR-ROUND WINTER

Size: 20" (50 cm)

Male: A plump gray duck with a brown head and a distinctive black rump. White belly and chestnut-tinged wings. Bright white wing linings. Small white wing patch, seen when swimming. Gray bill.

Female: similar to female Mallard, a mottled brown with a pronounced color change from dark brown body to light brown neck and head, bright white wing linings, small white wing patch, gray bill with orange sides

Juvenile: similar to female

Nest: ground; female lines the nest with fine grass and down feathers plucked from her chest; 1 brood per year

Eggs: 8-11; white without markings

Incubation: 24-27 days; female incubates

Fledging: 48-56 days; young feed themselves

Migration: complete to non-migrator in Texas

Food: aquatic insects

Compare: Male Gadwall is one of the few gray ducks. Look for its distinctive black rump.

Stan's Notes: A duck of shallow marshes. Consumes mostly plant material, dunking its head in water to feed rather than tipping forward, like other dabbling ducks. Walks well on land; feeds in fields and woodlands. Frequently in pairs with other duck species. Nests within 300 feet (100 m) of water. Establishes pair bond in winter.

juvenile

Yellow-crowned Night-Heron
Nyctanassa violacea

YEAR-ROUND
MIGRATION
SUMMER

Size: 24" (60 cm); up to 3½-foot wingspan

Male: Stocky gray heron with a black head, white crown and cheek patch. Dark thick bill and yellow legs. During breeding season, crown acquires a yellow hue.

Female: same as male

Juvenile: brown with white streaks and a dark bill, green legs

Nest: platform; female and male build; 1 brood per year

Eggs: 4-6; light blue without markings

Incubation: 21-25 days; female and male incubate

Fledging: 21-25 days; female and male feed young

Migration: complete to non-migrator in Texas

Food: aquatic insects, fish, crustaceans

Compare: One of several heron species in Texas. Distinctive patterned black and white head makes this heron easy to identify.

Stan's Notes: This heron hunts during the night, as the common name implies, but it can also be active during the day. Found in coastal mangroves to interior swamps, often hunting fiddler crabs and crayfish. Not uncommon for it to nest in large heron rookeries, and sometimes will nest by itself or in small colonies. Usually seen alone or in small groups. During the breeding season, the crown will acquire a yellow hue.

in flight

Canada Goose
Branta canadensis

WINTER

Size: 25-43" (63-109 cm); up to 5½-foot wingspan

Male: Large gray goose with black neck and head, with a white chin or cheek strap.

Female: same as male

Juvenile: same as adult

Nest: platform, on the ground; female constructs; 1 brood per year

Eggs: 5-10; white without markings

Incubation: 25-30 days; female incubates

Fledging: 42-55 days; male and female teach young to feed

Migration: partial migrator to complete, to Texas

Food: aquatic plants, insects, seeds

Compare: Large goose that is rarely confused with any other bird.

Stan's Notes: A winter bird throughout Texas with few year-round residents. Adults mate for many years, but only start to breed in their third year. Males often act as sentinels, standing at the edge of the group, bobbing their heads up and down, becoming very aggressive to anybody who approaches. Will hiss as if displaying displeasure. Adults molt their primary flight feathers while raising young, rendering family groups flightless at the same time. Several subspecies vary geographically across the U.S. Generally they are darker in color in western groups and paler in eastern. Size decreases northward, with the smallest subspecies found on the Arctic tundra.

in flight

rusty stain

rusty stain
in flight

Sandhill Crane
Grus canadensis

MIGRATION
WINTER

Size: 40-48" (102-120 cm); up to 7-foot wingspan

Male: Elegant gray bird with long legs and neck. Wings and body often stained rusty brown. Scarlet red cap. Yellow-to-red eyes.

Female: same as male

Juvenile: dull brown, lacks red cap, has yellow eyes

Nest: platform, on the ground; female and male build; 1 brood per year

Eggs: 2; olive with brown markings

Incubation: 28-32 days; female and male incubate

Fledging: 65 days; female and male feed young

Migration: complete, to Texas and Mexico

Food: insects, fruit, worms, plants, amphibians

Compare: Similar size as Great Blue Heron (pg. 315), but the Crane has a shorter bill and red cap. Great Blue Heron flies with neck held in an S shape unlike Crane's straight neck. The Whooping Crane (pg. 373) is taller with white plumage and a red mark behind bill.

Stan's Notes: Among the tallest birds in the world and capable of flying at great heights. Usually seen in large undisturbed fields near water. Has a very distinctive rattling call. Often heard before seen. Plumage often appears rusty brown (see insets) due to staining from mud during preening. A characteristic flight with upstroke quicker than down. Performing a spectacular mating dance, the birds face each other, bow and jump into the air while uttering loud cackling sounds and flapping wings. Often flips sticks and grass into the air during dance.

in flight

Great Blue Heron
Ardea herodias

Size: 42-52" (107-132 cm); up to 6-foot wingspan

Male: Tall gray heron. Black eyebrows extend into several long plumes off the back of head. Long yellow bill. Feathers at base of neck drop down in a kind of necklace.

Female: same as male

Juvenile: same as adult, but more brown than gray, with a black crown and no plumes

Nest: platform; male and female build; 1 brood per year

Eggs: 3-5; blue green without markings

Incubation: 27-28 days; female and male incubate

Fledging: 56-60 days; male and female feed young

Migration: non-migrator in Texas

Food: small fish, frogs, insects, snakes

Compare: Similar size as the Sandhill Crane (pg. 313), but lacks the Crane's red crown. Crane flies with neck held straight unlike the Heron's S-shaped neck. Tricolored Heron (pg. 105) is half the size and has a white belly.

Stan's Notes: One of the most common herons, often barking like a dog when startled. Seen stalking small fish in shallow water. Will strike at mice, squirrels and just about anything else it might come across. Flies holding neck in an S shape, with its long legs trailing straight out behind. The wings are held in cupped fashion during flight. Nests in colonies of up to 100 birds. Nests in treetops near or over open water. A year-round resident. Populations increase when birds north of Texas migrate to spend the winter.

male

female

SUMMER

Ruby-throated Hummingbird
Archilochus colubris

Size: 3-3½" (7.5-9 cm)

Male: Tiny iridescent green bird with black throat patch that reflects bright ruby red in sun.

Female: same as male, but lacking the throat patch

Juvenile: same as female

Nest: cup; female builds; 1-2 broods per year

Eggs: 2; white without markings

Incubation: 12-14 days; female incubates

Fledging: 14-18 days; female feeds young

Migration: complete, to Mexico and Central America

Food: nectar, insects; will come to nectar feeders

Compare: No other bird is as tiny. The Sphinx Moth also hovers at flowers, but has clear wings and a mouth part that looks like a straw, which coils up when not at flowers. Doesn't hum in flight, moves much slower than the Hummingbird and can be approached.

Stan's Notes: The smallest bird in the state. Able to hover, fly up and down, and is the only bird to fly backward. Does not sing, but will chatter or buzz to communicate. The wings create a humming noise, flapping 50-60 times each second or faster during chasing flights. The heart pumps an incredible 1,260 beats per minute, and it breathes 250 times per minute. Weighing just 2-3 grams, it takes about five average-sized hummingbirds to equal the weight of one chickadee. Constructs its nest with plant material and spider webs, gluing pieces of lichen on the outside for camouflage. Attracted to tubular red flowers.

Black-chinned Hummingbird

Archilochus alexandri

SUMMER

Size: 3¾" (9.5 cm)

Male: Tiny iridescent green bird with black throat patch (gorget) that reflects violet blue in sunlight. Black chin. White chest and belly.

Female: same as male, but lacking the throat patch and black chin, has white flanks

Juvenile: similar to female

Nest: cup; female builds; 1-2 broods per year

Eggs: 1-3; white without markings

Incubation: 13-16 days; female incubates

Fledging: 19-21 days; female feeds young

Migration: complete, to Central and South America

Food: nectar, insects; will come to nectar feeders

Compare: The male Ruby-throated (pg. 317) is similar, but it has a ruby red throat patch unlike the violet blue throat patch of the male Black-chinned. Male Black-chinned often appears to have an all-black head.

Stan's Notes: One of several hummingbird species in Texas. Can fly backward, but doesn't sing. Will chatter or buzz to communicate. Wings create a humming noise, flapping nearly 80 times per second. Weighing only 2-3 grams, it takes approximately five average-sized hummingbirds to equal the weight of one chickadee. Males return first at the end of April. Male performs a spectacular pendulum-like flight over a perched female. After mating, the female builds a nest, using spider webs to glue nest materials together, and raises young without mate's help. More than one clutch per year not uncommon.

male

female

Painted Bunting
Passerina ciris

SUMMER

Size: 5½" (14 cm)

Male: An amazing combination of colors. A green back, deep blue head and orange chest and belly. Dark wings and tail.

Female: bright green above, light green below

Juvenile: drab version of the female with only some small spots of green

Nest: cup; female and male construct; 1-2 broods per year

Eggs: 3-5; pale blue with brown markings

Incubation: 11-12 days; female incubate

Fledging: 12-14 days; female and male feed young

Migration: complete, to Mexico and Central America

Food: seeds, insects; will visit seed feeders

Compare: No other bird can compare with the male's striking colors. Female is uniquely green and rarely confused with any other bird.

Stan's Notes: A wonderful bird of backyard gardens, woodland edges and along brushy roads, it will visit seed feeders in wooded yards. Well known for its loud, clear and varied warbling phrases. Cup nest, made of grass and lined with animal hair, is often in a deep, tangled mass of vines. A common cowbird host, this usually unfortunately results in raising the cowbird young only and not its own. Often captured in Central America and sold as a caged bird; both activities are illegal in the U.S. and should not be supported.

MIGRATION
WINTER

Green-tailed Towhee
Pipilo chlorurus

Size: 7¼" (18.5 cm)

Male: A unique yellowish green back, wings and tail. Dark gray chest and face. Bright white throat with black stripes. Rusty red crown.

Female: same as male

Juvenile: olive green with heavy streaking on breast and belly, lacks crown and throat markings of adult

Nest: cup; female and male construct; 1-2 broods per year

Eggs: 3-5; white with brown markings

Incubation: 12-14 days; female and male incubate

Fledging: 10-14 days; female and male feed young

Migration: complete, to parts of Texas, Mexico, Central America

Food: insects, seeds, fruit

Compare: Smaller than Green Jay (pg. 325), which has a blue crown and black throat. Green-tailed's unusual color, short wings, long tail and large bill make it easy to identify.

Stan's Notes: Seen during migration and in winter in half of Texas. Found on shrubby hillsides and sagebrush mountain slopes up to 7,000 feet (2,150 m). Like other towhees, searches for insects and seeds, taking a little jump forward while kicking backward with both feet. Known to scurry away from trouble, jumping to ground without opening its wings and running across the ground.

Green Jay
Cyanocorax yncas

YEAR-ROUND

Size: 10½" (27 cm)

Male: Uniquely colored and patterned with a pale green body and wings, blue crown and face with a black chin, throat and upper breast. Yellow belly, wings, outer tail feathers and underside of tail.

Female: same as male

Juvenile: similar to adult, but not as brightly colored

Nest: cup; female and male construct; 1 brood per year

Eggs: 3-5; pale white to gray with brown marks

Incubation: 17-18 days; female and male incubate

Fledging: 18-22 days; female and male feed young

Migration: non-migrator; moves around to find food

Food: seeds, fruit, nectar, nuts, carrion, small mammals; comes to seed and fruit feeders

Compare: A unique bird with a combination of green, blue and yellow.

Stan's Notes: Tropical bird restricted to southern Texas in the U.S., but range extends to Central America. Also known as Rio Grande Jay. Travels in noisy family groups of up to ten or more. Found mainly in dense vegetation, with a small home territory. A strong flyer, often gliding between perches or to ground. Flashes bright yellow under wings in flight. An inquisitive, friendly bird, quickly investigating feeders or fruit. Caches food, burying acorns. Steals acorns from other birds. Only one pair breeds in a flock. Like other jays it has helpers, usually family members, to help raise the young. Two-year-old birds are dispersed from the family unit by parents.

female pg. 209

male

Wood Duck
Aix sponsa

YEAR-ROUND
SUMMER
WINTER

Size: 17-20" (43-50 cm)

Male: A small, highly ornamented dabbling duck with a green head and crest patterned with white and black. A rusty chest, white belly and red eyes.

Female: brown, similar size and shape as male, has bright white eye-ring and a not-so-obvious crest, blue patch on wing often hidden

Juvenile: same as female

Nest: cavity; female lines old woodpecker cavity; 1 brood per year

Eggs: 10-15; creamy white without markings

Incubation: 28-36 days; female incubates

Fledging: 56-68 days; female teaches young to feed

Migration: non-migrator to partial migrator in Texas

Food: aquatic insects, plants, seeds

Compare: More colorful than male Green-winged Teal (pg. 191). Smaller than the male Shoveler (pg. 333) and lacks the long wide bill.

Stan's Notes: A common duck of quiet, shallow backwater ponds. Nearly extinct around 1900 due to overhunting, but is doing well now. Nests in an old woodpecker hole or uses a nesting box. Often seen flying deep in forests or perched high on tree branches. Female takes to flight with a loud squealing call and enters nest cavity from full flight. Lays eggs in a neighboring female nest (egg dumping), resulting in some clutches in excess of 20 eggs. Young stay in nest 24 hours after hatching, then jump from up to 30 feet (9 m) to the ground or water to follow their mother, never returning to the nest.

YEAR-ROUND
SUMMER

Green Heron
Butorides virescens

Size: 16-22" (40-56 cm)

Male: Short stocky heron with a blue-green back and rusty red neck and chest. Dark green crest. Short legs, normally yellow, but turn bright orange during breeding season.

Female: same as male

Juvenile: similar to adult, with a blue-gray back and white-streaked chest and neck

Nest: platform; female and male build; 2 broods per year

Eggs: 2-4; light green without markings

Incubation: 21-25 days; female and male incubate

Fledging: 35-36 days; female and male feed young

Migration: complete to non-migrator, to coastal Texas, Mexico, Central and South America

Food: fish, insects, amphibians, aquatic plants

Compare: Green Heron is smaller than the Tricolored Heron (pg. 105) and lacks the long neck of most other herons. Also much smaller than the Great Blue Heron (pg. 315). Look for a small heron with a dark green back and crest stalking wetlands.

Stan's Notes: Often gives an explosive, rasping "skyew" call when startled. Sometimes it looks like it doesn't have a neck, because it holds its head close to its body. Hunts for small fish, aquatic insects and small amphibians by waiting on a shore or wading stealthily. Has been known to place an object such as an insect on the water surface to attract fish to catch. Raises its crest when excited.

female pg. 213

male

Mallard
Anas platyrhynchos

SUMMER
WINTER

Size: 19-21" (48-53 cm)

Male: Large, bulbous green head, white necklace and rust brown or chestnut chest. Gray and white on the sides. Yellow bill. Orange legs and feet.

Female: all brown with orange and black bill, small blue and white wing mark (speculum)

Juvenile: same as female, but with a yellow bill

Nest: ground; female builds; 1 brood per year

Eggs: 7-10; greenish to whitish, unmarked

Incubation: 26-30 days; female incubates

Fledging: 42-52 days; female leads young to food

Migration: complete, to Texas

Food: seeds, plants, aquatic insects; will come to ground feeders offering corn

Compare: The male Northern Shoveler (pg. 333) has a white chest with rust on sides and a dark spoon-shaped bill. Breeding male Northern Pintail (pg. 217) has long tail feathers and a brown head.

Stan's Notes: A familiar duck of lakes and ponds, it's considered a type of dabbling duck, tipping forward in shallow water to feed on aquatic plants on the bottom. The name "Mallard" comes from the Latin *masculus*, meaning "male," referring to the habit of males not taking part in raising ducklings. Black central tail feathers of male curl upward. Both the male and female have white tails and white underwings. Will return to place of birth.

female pg. 219

male

Northern Shoveler
Anas clypeata

WINTER

Size: 20" (50 cm)

Male: Medium-sized duck with iridescent green head, rusty sides and white breast. Has an extraordinarily large spoon-shaped bill that is almost always held pointed toward water.

Female: brown and black all over, green speculum, spoon-shaped bill

Juvenile: same as female

Nest: ground; female builds; 1 brood per year

Eggs: 9-12; olive without markings

Incubation: 22-25 days; female incubates

Fledging: 30-60 days; female leads young to food

Migration: complete, to Texas, Mexico, Central America

Food: aquatic insects, plants

Compare: Similar to the male Mallard (pg. 331), but Shoveler has a large, characteristic spoon-shaped bill. Larger than male Wood Duck (pg. 327) and lacks Wood Duck's crest.

Stan's Notes: One of several species of shoveler, so called because of the peculiar shape of its bill. The Northern Shoveler is the only species of these ducks in North America. Found in small flocks of 5-10, swimming low in water with its large bill pointed toward the water, as if it's too heavy to lift. Feeds mainly by filtering tiny aquatic insects and plants from the water's surface with its bill. Winters in Texas where it can find water.

male

female pg. 391

Baltimore Oriole
Icterus galbula

MIGRATION
SUMMER

Size: 7-8" (18-20 cm)

Male: Bright flaming orange bird with black head and black extending down nape of neck onto the back. Black wings with white and orange wing bars. An orange tail with black streaks. Gray bill and dark eyes.

Female: pale yellow with orange tones, gray brown wings, white wing bars, gray bill, dark eyes

Juvenile: same as female

Nest: pendulous; female builds; 1 brood per year

Eggs: 4-5; bluish with brown markings

Incubation: 12-14 days; female incubates

Fledging: 12-14 days; female and male feed young

Migration: complete, to Mexico, Central America and South America

Food: insects, fruit, nectar; comes to orange half and nectar feeders

Compare: The male Bullock's Oriole (pg. 339) lacks the black "hood." The male Orchard Oriole (pg. 337) is a much darker orange than the Baltimore's brighter flaming orange.

Stan's Notes: A fantastic songster, this bird is often heard before seen. Easily attracted to a feeder offering grape jelly, orange halves or sugar water (nectar). Parents bring young to feeders. Sits in tops of trees feeding on caterpillars. Female builds a sock-like nest at the outermost branches of tall trees. Often returns to the same area year after year. Some of the last birds to arrive in spring (May) and first to leave in fall (September).

female pg. 393

male

Orchard Oriole
Icterus spurius

SUMMER

Size: 7-8" (18-20 cm)

Male: Dull orange bird with black head and black extending down the back. A black chin, tail and wings. Single white wing bars. A long, thin black bill with a small gray mark on lower mandible (jaw).

Female: olive green back with a dull yellow belly, 2 white wing bars on dark gray wings

Juvenile: same as female, black bib on first-year male

Nest: pendulous; female builds; 1 brood per year

Eggs: 3-5; pale blue to white, brown markings

Incubation: 11-12 days; female and male incubate

Fledging: 11-14 days; female and male feed young

Migration: complete, to Mexico, Central America and northern South America

Food: insects, fruit; comes to fruit/nectar feeders

Compare: Similar to male Baltimore Oriole (pg. 335), but the male Orchard Oriole has a much darker orange body.

Stan's Notes: Prefers orchards or open woods, hence its common name. Eats insects until wild fruit starts to ripen. One of the last birds to arrive in spring and one of the first to leave in fall. Spends 4-5 months in Texas. Frequently migrates with the more abundant Baltimore Oriole. Usually nests alone, but sometimes nests in small colonies. Parents bring the young to jelly and orange half feeders shortly after fledging. Many people mistakenly think the orioles have left during summer but, in fact, these birds are concentrating on finding insects to feed their young.

female pg. 395

male

Bullock's Oriole
Icterus bullockii

SUMMER

Size: 8" (20 cm)

Male: Bright orange and black bird. Black crown, eye line, nape, chin, back and wings with a bold white patch on wings.

Female: dull yellow overall, pale white belly, white wing bars on gray-to-black wings

Juvenile: similar to female

Nest: pendulous; female and male build; 1 brood per year

Eggs: 4-6; pale white to gray, brown markings

Incubation: 12-14 days; female incubates

Fledging: 12-14 days; female and male feed young

Migration: complete, to Central and South America

Food: insects, berries, nectar; visits nectar feeders

Compare: A handsome bird. Lacks the black "hood" of the male Baltimore Oriole (pg. 335). Male Hooded Oriole (pg. 341) is the same size, but lacks the black crown and nape. Look for Bullock's bright markings, and a thin black line running through each eye.

Stan's Notes: So closely related to Baltimore Orioles of the eastern U.S., at one time both were considered a single species. Interbreeds with Baltimores where their ranges overlap. Most common in the state where cottonwood trees grow along rivers and other wetlands. Also found at edges of clearings, in city parks, on farms and along irrigation ditches. Hanging sock-like nest is constructed of plant fibers such as inner bark of junipers and willows. Will incorporate yarn and thread into its nest if offered at the time of nest building.

female pg. 397

male

Hooded Oriole
Icterus cucullatus

Size: 8" (20 cm)

Male: Orange yellow head, nape, chest, rump and belly. Black face, chin, throat, bill and eyes. Large white wing bar. Dark wings and tail.

Female: dull yellow with gray wings and back

Juvenile: similar to adult of the same sex

Nest: pendulous; female and male construct; 1-2 broods per year

Eggs: 3-5; dull white with brown markings

Incubation: 12-14 days; female incubates

Fledging: 12-14 days; female and male feed young

Migration: complete, to Central and South America

Food: insects, fruit, nectar

Compare: Male Bullock's Oriole (pg. 339) is the same size, but has a black crown and nape. Male Scott's Oriole (pg. 401) is larger and has a black head and chest.

Stan's Notes: A bird of tree-lined creeks and streams, palm groves, mesquite and arid scrub, often near suburbs. Male courts female with bows while hopping around her, singing a soft song. Points his bill skyward (like many birds in the blackbird family). Female will respond with a similar dance. Constructs an unusual sock-like nest, hung from a twig or woven through a palm leaf. Entrance often near the top, but can be on the side. Takes 3-7 days to build nest of wiry green grass, shredded palm leaves or yucca fibers. Some repair and reuse nests. Sips flower nectar, but not like hummingbirds. Often slices into the base of a flower, bypassing its natural entrance. Young are fed a regurgitate of insects and nectar the first 5-7 days of life.

SUMMER

female pg. 147

male

MIGRATION
SUMMER

Black-headed Grosbeak

Pheucticus melanocephalus

Size: 8" (20 cm)

Male: Stocky bird with burnt orange chest, neck and rump. Black head, tail and wings with irregular-shaped white wing patches. Large bill with upper bill darker than lower.

Female: appears like an overgrown sparrow, overall brown with a lighter breast and belly, large two-toned bill, prominent white eyebrows, yellow wing linings, as seen in flight

Juvenile: similar to adult of the same sex

Nest: cup; female builds; 1 brood per year

Eggs: 3-4; pale green or bluish, brown markings

Incubation: 11-13 days; female and male incubate

Fledging: 11-13 days; female and male feed young

Migration: complete, to Mexico, Central America and South America

Food: seeds, insects, fruit; comes to seed feeders

Compare: The male Bullock's Oriole (pg. 339) has more white on wings than the male Black-headed. Look for Black-headed's large bicolored bill.

Stan's Notes: A cosmopolitan bird that nests in a wide variety of habitats. Both the male and female sing and will aggressively defend the nest against intruders. Song is very similar to American Robin's, making it hard to tell them apart by song. Populations increasing in Texas and across the U.S.

male

female pg. 113

yellow male

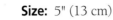

House Finch
Carpodacus mexicanus

YEAR-ROUND

Size: 5" (13 cm)

Male: An orange red face, breast and rump, with a brown cap. Brown marking behind eyes. Brown wings streaked with white. A white belly with brown streaks.

Female: brown with a heavily streaked white chest

Juvenile: similar to female

Nest: cup, sometimes in cavities; female builds; 2 broods per year

Eggs: 4-5; pale blue, lightly marked

Incubation: 12-14 days; female incubates

Fledging: 15-19 days; female and male feed young

Migration: non-migrator; moves around to find food

Food: seeds, fruit, leaf buds; will visit seed feeders

Compare: The male Vermilion Flycatcher (pg. 347) has a black nape, back and wings.

Stan's Notes: Very social bird. Visits feeders in small flocks. Likes nesting in hanging flower baskets. Incubating female fed by male. Loud, cheerful warbling song. Suffers a fatal eye disease that causes eyes to crust over. Historically it occurred from the Pacific coast to the Rocky Mountains, with a few reaching the eastern side. Birds introduced to Long Island, New York, in the 1940s have populated the entire eastern U.S. Now found throughout the U.S. Can be the most common bird at your feeders. Rarely, some males are yellow (see inset) instead of red, probably due to poor diet.

female pg. 265

male

Vermilion Flycatcher
Pyrocephalus rubinus

SUMMER
WINTER

Size: 6" (15 cm)

Male: A stunningly beautiful bird with a crimson red head, crest, chin, breast and belly. Black nape, back, wings and tail. Thick black line running through eyes. Thin black bill.

Female: gray head, neck and back, nearly white chin and breast, pink belly to undertail, black tail, thin black bill

Juvenile: similar to female, lacks a pink undertail

Nest: cup; female builds; 1-2 broods per year

Eggs: 2-4; white with brown markings

Incubation: 14-16 days; female and male incubate

Fledging: 14-16 days; female and male feed young

Migration: complete, to Mexico

Food: insects (mainly bees)

Compare: The unique bright crimson plumage with black wings make this bird easy to identify.

Stan's Notes: A uniquely colored flycatcher with few staying all winter in extreme southern Texas. Often found in open areas with shrubs and small trees close to water. Feeds mainly on insects, with bees making up a large part of its diet. Will perch on a thin branch, pumping tail up and down while waiting for an aerial insect. Flies out to snatch it, then returns to the perch. Drops to the ground for terrestrial insects. Male raises its crest, fluffs chest feathers, fans tail and sings a song during a fluttery flight to court females. Female builds a shallow nest of twigs and grasses and lines it with downy plant material. Male feeds female during incubation and brooding.

female
pg. 399

male

Summer Tanager
Piranga rubra

Size: 8" (20 cm)

Male: Bright rosy red bird with darker red wings.

Female: overall yellow with slightly darker wings

Juvenile: male has patches of red and green over the entire body, female is same as adult female

Nest: cup; female builds; 1-2 broods per year

Eggs: 3-5; pale blue with dark markings

Incubation: 10-12 days; female incubates

Fledging: unknown days; female and male feed young

Migration: complete, to Central and South America

Food: insects, fruit

Compare: Similar size as the male Northern Cardinal (pg. 351), but Cardinal has a black mask, large crest and red bill.

Stan's Notes: Found in Texas where woodlands exist, especially in mixed pine and oak forests. Due to land clearing for agriculture, populations have decreased over the past century and especially during the last two decades. Returning to Texas in late April and with young hatching in late May, some pairs have two broods per year. While fruit makes up some of the diet, most of it consists of insects such as bees and wasps. Summer Tanagers unfortunately seem to be parasitized by Brown-headed Cowbirds.

female pg. 159

male

juvenile

Northern Cardinal
Cardinalis cardinalis

YEAR-ROUND

Size: 8-9" (20-22.5 cm)

Male: All-red bird with a black mask that extends from the face down to the chin and throat. Large red bill and crest.

Female: buff brown with tinges of red on crest and wings, same black mask and red bill

Juvenile: same as female, but with a blackish gray bill

Nest: cup; female builds; 2-3 broods per year

Eggs: 3-4; bluish white with brown markings

Incubation: 12-13 days; female and male incubate

Fledging: 9-10 days; female and male feed young

Migration: non-migrator

Food: seeds, insects, fruit; comes to seed feeders

Compare: Similar size as the male Summer Tanager (pg. 349), but Tanager is rosy red. Look for Northern Cardinal's black mask, large crest and red bill.

Stan's Notes: A familiar backyard bird. Look for the male feeding female during courtship. Male feeds young of the first brood by himself while female builds second nest. The name comes from the Latin word *cardinalis*, which means "important." Very territorial in spring, it will fight its own reflection in a window. Non-territorial during winter, gathering in small flocks of up to 20 birds. Both the male and female sing and can be heard anytime of year. Listen for its "whata-cheer-cheer-cheer" territorial call in the spring.

female pg. 211

male

Redhead
Aythya americana

Size: 19" (48 cm)

Male: Rich red head and neck with a black breast and tail. Gray sides. Smoky gray wings and back. Tricolored bill with a light blue base, white ring and black tip.

Female: plain, soft brown duck with gray-to-white wing linings, top of head rounded, gray bill with black tip

Juvenile: similar to female

Nest: cup; female builds; 1 brood per year

Eggs: 9-14; pale white without markings

Incubation: 24-28 days; female and male incubate

Fledging: 56-73 days; female shows the young what to eat

Migration: complete, to Texas

Food: seeds, aquatic plants, insects

Compare: The male Northern Shoveler (pg. 333) has a green head and rusty sides unlike the male Redhead's gray sides.

Stan's Notes: A duck of permanent large bodies of water. Forages along the shoreline, feeding on seeds, aquatic plants and insects. Usually builds nest directly on surface of water, using large mats of vegetation. Female lays up to 75 percent of its eggs in the nests of other Redheads and several other duck species. Nests primarily in the Prairie Pothole region of the northern Great Plains. The overall populations seem to be increasing at about 2-3 percent each year. Winters throughout Texas where it can find water.

juvenile

in flight

Roseate Spoonbill

Platalea ajaja

YEAR-ROUND
SUMMER

Size: 32" (80 cm); up to 4-foot wingspan

Male: An overall pink bird with red highlights. A white neck with a black patch on the back of the head. A heavy, spoon-shaped flat bill. Long red legs.

Female: same as male

Juvenile: pale version of adult

Nest: platform; female and male build; 1 brood per year

Eggs: 1-4; olive green with dark markings

Incubation: 22-23 days; male and female incubate

Fledging: 35-42 days; female and male feed young

Migration: partial migrator to non-migrator

Food: fish, aquatic insects, snails, worms, leeches

Compare: An unmistakable bird of Texas. Larger than the White Ibis (pg. 367), which has a long, down-curved orange-to-red bill unlike the heavy flat bill of the Spoonbill.

Stan's Notes: A summer resident in eastern parts of Texas and a year-round Gulf coast resident. This bird is making a comeback from devastating hunting pressures during the 1800s for its wing feathers, which were used in women's hats and fans. Now habitat destruction is limiting its numbers. Swings its spoon-shaped bill to sift fish and insects from shallow waters. Usually found in small flocks. Nests in mixed colonies with herons. Related to the ibises.

in flight

breeding

in flight

winter

YEAR-ROUND

Laughing Gull
Larus atricilla

Size: 16-17" (40-43 cm); up to 3½-foot wingspan

Male: Breeding adult has a black head "hood" and white neck, chest and belly. Slate gray back and wings with black wing tips. Orange bill. Incomplete white eye-ring. Winter plumage lacks the "hood" and has a black bill.

Female: same as male

Juvenile: brown throughout, gray sides, lacking the black head and white chest, has a gray bill

Nest: ground; male and female construct; 1 brood per year

Eggs: 2-4; olive with brown markings

Incubation: 18-20 days; female and male incubate

Fledging: 30-35 days; male and female feed young

Migration: non-migrator along coastal Texas

Food: fish, insects, aquatic insects

Compare: Smaller than the Ring-billed Gull (pg. 359). Look for black head "hood" and slate gray back and wings of Laughing Gull.

Stan's Notes: This is a three-year gull that starts out mostly brown and gray. The second year it resembles adults, but lacks a complete black head "hood." Breeding plumage in the third year. Male tosses its head back and calls to attract a mate. Nests in marshes in large colonies. Nest is a scrape on the ground lined with grass, sticks and rocks. Adults feed young a half-digested regurgitant.

winter

in flight

breeding

juvenile

YEAR-ROUND
WINTER

Ring-billed Gull
Larus delawarensis

Size: 19" (48 cm); up to 4-foot wingspan

Male: A white bird with gray wings, black wing tips spotted with white, and a white tail, as seen in flight. Yellow bill with a black ring near tip. Yellowish legs and feet. Winter or non-breeding adult has a speckled brown back of head and nape of neck.

Female: same as male

Juvenile: mostly gray version of winter adult, has a dark band at end of tail

Nest: ground; female and male construct; 1 brood per year

Eggs: 2-4; off-white with brown markings

Incubation: 20-21 days; female and male incubate

Fledging: 20-40 days; female and male feed young

Migration: complete to non-migrator in Texas

Food: insects, fish; scavenges for food

Compare: Larger than the Laughing Gull (pg. 357) and lacks the black head "hood." Look for a large white gull with a black ring around the bill near the tip.

Stan's Notes: A common gull of garbage dumps and parking lots. It's expanding its range and remaining farther north longer during winter due to successful scavenging in cities. A three-year gull with a new, different plumage in each of the first three autumns. Attains ring on bill after its first winter and adult plumage in its third year. Defends a small area around nest.

Cattle Egret
Bubulcus ibis

YEAR-ROUND
SUMMER

Size: 20" (50 cm); up to 3-foot wingspan

Male: Stocky with a disproportional large round head. White with orange buff crest, breast and back. Red-orange bill and legs. Winter plumage is all white with a yellow bill and dark legs.

Female: same as male

Juvenile: similar to winter adult, with a dark bill

Nest: platform; female and male build; 1 brood per year

Eggs: 2-5; light blue green without markings

Incubation: 22-26 days; female and male incubate

Fledging: 28-30 days; female and male feed young

Migration: partial migrator to non-migrator in Texas; moves around to find food

Food: insects, small mammals

Compare: About half the size of Great Egret (pg. 371), which has a much longer neck and a much larger bill. White Ibis (pg. 367) has a large down-curved bill.

Stan's Notes: Came to South America from Africa around 1880, reaching Florida in the 1940s. Started being seen in Texas in the mid-1950s. Often seen singularly in pastures, hunting insects at cow and horse pies. Holding its head still while wiggling its neck back and forth and from side to side, it stabs at prey, captures it, then tosses it to the back of its mouth in one swift move. Frequently attracted to field fires to hunt newly exposed animals and insects. In some years it is found as far as northern tier states and Canada.

winter

in flight

breeding

Caspian Tern

Sterna caspia

YEAR-ROUND

Size: 21" (53 cm); up to 4-foot wingspan

Male: White chest and belly. White wing surfaces below and light gray above, with black tips, as seen in flight. Light gray back. Black cap extends over eyes. Large dark red bill with darker tip. Black legs. Winter plumage has a streaked cap.

Female: same as male

Juvenile: similar to winter adult, orange bill

Nest: ground; female and male construct; 1 brood per year

Eggs: 1-4; pinkish with brown markings

Incubation: 20-22 days; female and male incubate

Fledging: 30-40 days; female and male feed young

Migration: non-migrator along coastal Texas

Food: fish, aquatic insects

Compare: Smaller and more streamlined than most gulls, with thinner wings than gull wings. Look for the large red bill and black cap.

Stan's Notes: A large strong tern with a deep, harsh loud scream. Frequently seen in large groups flying at about 30 feet (9 m) above water, patrolling for fish. Nests in large colonies on small islands and sand beaches. The young recognize the calls of their parents, which helps them find each other when adults return to the colony with food. Young chase adults until they are fed. Adults feed young for up to seven months, the longest time of any tern species.

in flight

YEAR-ROUND
MIGRATION
SUMMER

Snowy Egret
Egretta thula

Size: 24" (60 cm); up to 3½-foot wingspan

Male: All-white bird. Black bill. Black legs. Bright yellow feet. Long feather plumes on head, neck and back during breeding season.

Female: same as male

Juvenile: similar to adult, but backs of legs are yellow

Nest: platform; female and male build; 1 brood per year

Eggs: 3-5; light blue-green without markings

Incubation: 20-24 days; female and male incubate

Fledging: 28-30 days; female and male feed young

Migration: partial migrator to non-migrator in Texas

Food: aquatic insects, small fish

Compare: Much smaller than Great Egret (pg. 371), which has a yellow bill and black feet. Look for the black bill and yellow feet of Snowy Egret to help identify. Same size as juvenile Little Blue Heron (pg. 103), which has a black-tipped gray bill.

Stan's Notes: Common in wetlands and often seen with other egrets. Colonies may include up to several hundred nests. Nests are low in shrubs 5-10 feet (1.5-3 m) tall or are on the ground, usually mixed among other egret and heron nests. Chicks hatch days apart (asynchronous), leading to starvation of last to hatch. Will actively "hunt" prey by moving around quickly, stirring up small fish and aquatic insects with its feet. In the breeding state, a yellow patch at the base of bill and the yellow feet turn orange-red. Was hunted to near extinction in the late 1800s for its feathers.

juvenile

White Ibis
Eudocimus albus

YEAR-ROUND

Size: 25" (63 cm); up to 3-foot wingspan

Male: All-white bird with a very long, downward curving orange-to-red bill. Pink facial skin. Leg color matches bill. Black wing tips, seen only in flight.

Female: same as male, but smaller, downward curve of bill is less than curve of male bill

Juvenile: combination of chocolate brown and white for the first two years, dull orange bill

Nest: platform; female and male build; 1 brood per year

Eggs: 2-3; light blue with dark markings

Incubation: 21-23 days; female and male incubate

Fledging: 28-35 days; female and male feed young

Migration: non-migrator along coastal Texas

Food: aquatic insects, crustaceans, fish

Compare: One of two ibis species regularly found in Texas. The White Ibis is completely white, unlike the slightly smaller, brown White-faced Ibis (pg. 235). Look for the long down-curved bill to help identify the Ibis.

Stan's Notes: Has been increasing in Texas over the past 50 years, with inland sightings getting more common. A year-round resident along the coast. Prefers fresh water over salt water, with crayfish a big part of its diet. White plumage with black wing tips and a bright orange-to-red down-curved bill make this species easy to identify. Often seen flying in groups of 30 or more. Nests in large colonies in well-made stick nests.

blue morph

juvenile

white
morph

Ross's Goose

in flight

Snow Goose
Chen caerulescens

Size: 25-38" (63-96 cm); up to 4½-foot wingspan

Male: A mostly white goose with varying patches of black and brown. Black wing tips. Pink bill and legs. Some individuals are grayish with a white head.

Female: same as male

Juvenile: overall dull gray with a dark bill

Nest: ground; female builds; 1 brood per year

Eggs: 3-5; white without markings

Incubation: 23-25 days; female incubates

Fledging: 45-49 days; female and male teach young to feed

Migration: complete, to coastal Texas, Mexico

Food: aquatic insects and plants

Compare: Canada Goose (pg. 311) has a black neck and white chin strap. The American White Pelican (pg. 375) shares black wing tips, but has an enormous bill.

Stan's Notes: Two color morphs. The more common white morph is pure white with black wing tips. Gray morph is often called blue, with a white head, gray chest and back and pink bill and legs. Has a thick serrated bill for pulling up plants. Breeds in large colonies on tundra of northern Canada. Females start breeding at 2-3 years. Older females produce more eggs and are more successful than the younger females. Seen by the thousands during migration and in winter. Very similar to the Ross's Goose (see inset), which is slightly smaller and has a much smaller pink bill. Commonly seen with Ross's Geese and Sandhill Cranes.

in flight

YEAR-ROUND

Great Egret
Ardea alba

Size: 38" (96 cm); up to 4½-foot wingspan

Male: Tall, thin, elegant all-white bird with long, pointed yellow bill. Black stilt-like legs and black feet.

Female: same as male

Juvenile: same as adult

Nest: platform; male and female build; 1 brood per year

Eggs: 2-3; light blue without markings

Incubation: 23-26 days; female and male incubate

Fledging: 43-49 days; female and male feed young

Migration: non-migrator in eastern Texas

Food: fish, aquatic insects, frogs, crayfish

Compare: Cattle Egret (pg. 361) is about half the size of Great Egret and has a much shorter neck and much smaller bill. The Snowy Egret (pg. 365) is much smaller with yellow feet and a black bill. Great Blue Heron (pg. 315) has a similar shape, but is larger in size and is not white. White Ibis (pg. 367) has a very long, downward curving orange-to-red bill.

Stan's Notes: A tall and stately bird, the Great Egret slowly stalks shallow wetlands looking for small fish to spear with its long sharp bill. Nests in colonies of up to 100 birds. Now protected, they were hunted to near extinction in the 1800s and early 1900s for their long white plumage. The name "Egret" came from the French word *aigrette*, which means "ornamental tufts of plumes." The plumes grow near the tail during breeding season.

Whooping Crane
Grus americana

MIGRATION
WINTER

Size: 51-53" (130-135 cm); up to 7¼-ft. wingspan

Male: White bird with a distinctive red crown and red patch just behind the bill (malar mark). Long dark legs. A long, pointed yellow bill. Black wing tips, seen in flight.

Female: same as male

Juvenile: similar to adult, tan to cinnamon brown, turns white during first winter

Nest: ground; female and male construct; 1 brood per year

Eggs: 1-3; cream to white with brown markings

Incubation: 29-31 days; female and male incubate

Fledging: 80-90 days; female and male feed young

Migration: complete, to coastal Texas

Food: insects, fruit, fish, small mammals, seeds

Compare: Sandhill Crane (pg. 313) is gray and lacks the malar mark. White Pelican (pg. 375) is smaller and holds head near body in flight.

Stan's Notes: The tallest bird in North America, but weighs only 10-15 pounds (5-7 kg). The Whooper is the rarest of 15 crane species worldwide and one of only two native to North America. An endangered crane with only 15 birds remaining in 1949. Almost always in marshy habitats in family groups of three or more. Can fly up to 50 miles (80 km) per hour. Takes off by running into wind with wings outstretched. Wingspan equal to or slightly larger than Bald Eagle. Matures at 4-6 years and can live 25 years or more. Thought to mate for life. Mated pairs defend territory of 30-50 acres (12-20 ha). Migrates to northern Canada to nest and raise young.

breeding

in flight

chick-feeding adult

YEAR-ROUND
MIGRATION

American White Pelican
Pelecanus erythrorhynchos

Size: 62" (158 cm); up to 9-foot wingspan

Male: A large white bird with black wing tips that extend partially down the trailing edge of wings. A white or pale yellow crown. Bright yellow bill, legs and feet. Breeding adult has a bright orange bill and legs. An adult that is feeding chicks (chick-feeding adult) has a gray-black crown.

Female: same as male

Juvenile: duller white with brownish head and neck

Nest: ground, a scraped-out depression rimmed with dirt; female and male build; 1 brood per year

Eggs: 1-3; white without markings

Incubation: 29-36 days; male and female incubate

Fledging: 60-70 days; female and male feed young

Migration: complete to non-migrator in Texas

Food: fish

Compare: Very similar to the Brown Pelican (pg. 243), only white with a yellow or orange bill.

Stan's Notes: Often seen in large groups on the larger lakes and reservoirs of Texas. They feed by simultaneously dipping their bills into water to scoop up fish. They don't dive into water to catch fish, like coastal Brown Pelicans. Bills and legs of breeding adults turn deep orange. Breeding adults usually also grow a flat fibrous plate in the middle of the upper mandible. This plate drops off after the eggs have hatched. They fly in a large V shape, often gliding with long wings, then all flapping together.

Lesser Goldfinch
Carduelis psaltria

YEAR-ROUND

Size: 4½" (11 cm)

Male: Striking bright yellow beneath from chin to base of tail. Black head, back, tail and wings with white patches on wings.

Female: dull yellow underneath, lacks a black head and back

Juvenile: same as female

Nest: cup; female builds; 1-2 broods per year

Eggs: 4-5; pale blue without markings

Incubation: 10-12 days; female incubates

Fledging: 12-14 days; female and male feed young

Migration: partial migrator to non-migrator; will move around the state to find food

Food: seeds, insects; will come to seed feeders

Compare: The male American Goldfinch (pg. 379) is slightly larger and has a yellow back unlike the black back of male Lesser Goldfinch.

Stan's Notes: Eastern range (Texas) males have black heads and backs, while western males have greenish backs. Some females are extremely pale. Prefers forest edges or places with short trees and a consistent water source. Unlike many other birds, its diet is about 96 percent seed, even during peak insect season. Will come to seed feeders. Late summer nesters. Male feeds the incubating female by regurgitating partially digested seeds. Pairs stay together all winter. Winter flocks can number in the hundreds.

winter male

male

female

WINTER

American Goldfinch
Carduelis tristis

Size: 5" (13 cm)

Male: A perky yellow bird with a black patch on forehead. Black tail with conspicuous white rump. Black wings with white wing bars. No marking on the chest. Dramatic change in color during winter, similar to female.

Female: dull olive yellow without a black forehead, with brown wings and a white rump

Juvenile: same as female

Nest: cup; female builds; 1 brood per year

Eggs: 4-6; pale blue without markings

Incubation: 10-12 days; female incubates

Fledging: 11-17 days; female and male feed young

Migration: non-migrator to partial migrator; flocks of up to 20 move around North America

Food: seeds, insects; will come to seed feeders

Compare: The male Lesser Goldfinch (pg. 377) has a black back. The Pine Siskin (pg. 111) and female House Finch (pg. 113) both have streaked chests. The male Wilson's Warbler (pg. 381) lacks black wings.

Stan's Notes: Most often found in open fields, scrubby areas and woodlands. Often called Wild Canary. A feeder bird that enjoys Nyjer thistle. Late summer nesting, uses the silky down from wild thistle for nest. Appears roller-coaster-like in flight. Listen for it to twitter during flight. Almost always in small flocks.

female

male

Wilson's Warbler
Wilsonia pusilla

MIGRATION
WINTER

Size: 4¾" (12 cm)

Male: Dull yellow upper and bright yellow lower. Distinctive black cap. Large black eyes and small thin bill.

Female: same as male, but lacking the black cap

Juvenile: similar to female

Nest: cup; female builds; 1 brood per year

Eggs: 4-6; white with brown markings

Incubation: 10-13 days; female incubates

Fledging: 8-11 days; female and male feed young

Migration: complete, to coastal Texas

Food: insects

Compare: Male American Goldfinch (pg. 379) has a black forehead and black wings. The male Common Yellowthroat (pg. 383) has a very distinctive black mask.

Stan's Notes: A widespread warbler seen during migration and in winter. Can be found near water in willow and alder thickets. Its all-insect diet makes it one of the top insect-eating birds in North America. Often flicks its tail and spreads its wings when hopping among thick shrubs, looking for insects. Females often mate with males that have the best territories and that might already have mates (polygyny).

male

female

Common Yellowthroat

Geothlypis trichas

YEAR-ROUND
MIGRATION
SUMMER
WINTER

Size: 5" (13 cm)

Male: Olive brown bird with bright yellow throat and breast, a white belly and a distinctive black mask outlined in white. A long, thin, pointed black bill.

Female: similar to male, lacks the black mask

Juvenile: same as female

Nest: cup; female builds; 2 broods per year

Eggs: 3-5; white with brown markings

Incubation: 11-12 days; female incubates

Fledging: 10-11 days; female and male feed young

Migration: complete to non-migrator in Texas

Food: insects

Compare: Found in a similar habitat as the American Goldfinch (pg. 379), but lacks the male's black forehead and wings. Yellow-rumped Warbler (pg. 257) has only spots of yellow. Male Wilson's Warbler (pg. 381) lacks the male Yellowthroat's black mask.

Stan's Notes: A common warbler of open fields and marshes. Has a cheerful, well-known song, "witchity-witchity-witchity-witchity." The male performs a curious courtship display, bouncing in and out of tall grass while uttering an unusual song. The young remain dependent upon the parents longer than most warblers. A frequent cowbird host. Becomes more abundant in winter when northern birds migrate to Texas. Usually quiet and secretive during winter.

Orange-crowned Warbler
Vermivora celata

MIGRATION
SUMMER
WINTER

Size: 5" (13 cm)

Male: An overall pale yellow bird with a dark line through eyes. Faint streaking on sides and chest. Small thin bill. Tawny orange crown, often invisible.

Female: same as male, but very slightly duller, often indistinguishable in the field

Juvenile: same as adults

Nest: cup; female builds; 1-2 broods per year

Eggs: 3-6; white with brown markings

Incubation: 12-14 days; female incubates

Fledging: 8-10 days; female and male feed young

Migration: complete, to Texas, Mexico, Central America

Food: insects, fruit, nectar

Compare: Male Common Yellowthroat (pg. 383) has a distinctive black mask. Wilson's Warbler (pg. 381) is brighter yellow with a distinct black cap.

Stan's Notes: This bird is often seen more during migration when large groups move together. Builds a bulky, well-concealed nest on the ground with nest rim at ground level. Known to feed at sapsucker taps and drink flower nectar. The orange crown tends to be hidden and is rarely seen in the field. A widespread breeder, from western Texas to Alaska and across Canada.

Pine Warbler
Dendroica pinus

YEAR-ROUND
WINTER

Size: 5½" (14 cm)

Male: A yellow throat and breast with faint black streaks on sides of breast. Olive green back. Two white wing bars. White belly.

Female: similar to male, only paler

Juvenile: similar to adults, but is browner with more white on belly

Nest: cup; female builds; 2-3 broods per year

Eggs: 3-5; white with brown markings

Incubation: 10-12 days; female incubates

Fledging: 12-14 days; female and male feed young

Migration: non-migrator to partial migrator in Texas

Food: insects, seeds, fruit

Compare: Similar size as the Yellow-rumped Warbler (pg. 257), but lacks a yellow rump. Similar size as the American Goldfinch (pg. 379), which lacks streaks on the breast.

Stan's Notes: Common resident of pine forests in the eastern half of the state. Builds nest only in pine forest. Brighter in spring and more drab in autumn, it varies in color depending on the time of year. Thought to have a larger bill than other warblers. Sometimes it is easier to identify by song than sight. Listen for a twittering, musical song that varies in speed.

male

female

MIGRATION
SUMMER

Dickcissel
Spiza americana

Size: 6" (15 cm)

Male: A small thick-billed bird with yellow chest, belly and eyebrows, and chestnut wings. A distinctive black bib under a white chin.

Female: same as male, but lacking the black bib

Juvenile: similar to female, only duller overall

Nest: cup, made of plant stems, grass and leaves; female builds; 1 brood per year

Eggs: 4-6; pale blue without markings

Incubation: 12-13 days; female incubates

Fledging: 9-11 days; female feeds young

Migration: complete, to Mexico, Central America and South America

Food: insects, seeds

Compare: The Western Meadowlark (pg. 405) is larger and has a prominent black V-shaped necklace unlike the Dickcissel's black bib.

Stan's Notes: Originally a bird of the prairie, now found in alfalfa fields, abandoned fields and meadows due to the loss of native prairie habitat. Prefers habitat that is sparsely vegetative. Doesn't do well in thick, dense vegetation. The males arrive at breeding sites a couple weeks before the females and begin to sing from prominent perches. Often seen singing from a fence post because it's the tallest object around. Nest is bulky, only a couple feet above ground and usually well concealed. Common name comes from an imitation of its song.

male pg. 335

female

Baltimore Oriole
Icterus galbula

MIGRATION
SUMMER

Size: 7-8" (18-20 cm)

Female: A pale yellow bird with orange tones, gray brown wings, white wing bars, a gray bill and dark eyes.

Male: bright flaming orange bird with black head and black extending down nape of neck onto the back, black wings with white and orange wing bars, an orange tail with black streaks, gray bill and dark eyes

Juvenile: same as female

Nest: pendulous; female builds; 1 brood per year

Eggs: 4-5; bluish with brown markings

Incubation: 12-14 days; female incubates

Fledging: 12-14 days; female and male feed young

Migration: complete, to Mexico, Central America and South America

Food: insects, fruit, nectar; comes to orange half and nectar feeders

Compare: Very similar to the female Orchard Oriole (pg. 393), which lacks orange tones and has less pronounced wing bars.

Stan's Notes: A fantastic songster, this bird is often heard before seen. Easily attracted to a feeder offering grape jelly, orange halves or sugar water (nectar). Parents bring young to feeders. Sits in tops of trees feeding on caterpillars. Female builds a sock-like nest at the outermost branches of tall trees. Often returns to the same area year after year. Some of the last birds to arrive in spring (May) and first to leave in fall (September).

male pg. 337

female

Orchard Oriole
Icterus spurius

Size: 7-8" (18-20 cm)

Female: An olive green bird with a dull yellow belly. Has 2 white wing bars on dark gray wings. Long, thin black bill with a small gray mark on lower mandible (jaw).

Male: dull orange with a black head, chin, upper back, wings and tail, single white wing bars

Juvenile: same as female, black bib on first-year male

Nest: pendulous; female builds; 1 brood per year

Eggs: 3-5; pale blue to white, brown markings

Incubation: 11-12 days; female and male incubate

Fledging: 11-14 days; female and male feed young

Migration: complete, to Mexico, Central America and northern South America

Food: insects, fruit; comes to fruit/nectar feeders

Compare: Female Baltimore Oriole (pg. 391) is similar, but has orange tones and more distinct wing bars. Female Summer Tanager (pg. 399) is mustard yellow with a larger bill.

Stan's Notes: Prefers orchards or open woods, hence its common name. Eats insects until wild fruit starts to ripen. One of the last birds to arrive in spring and one of the first to leave in fall. Spends 4-5 months in Texas. Frequently migrates with the more abundant Baltimore Oriole. Usually nests alone, but sometimes nests in small colonies. Parents bring young to jelly and orange half feeders just after fledging. Many think the orioles have left in summer, but the birds are concentrating on finding insects to feed their young.

male pg. 339

female

Bullock's Oriole
Icterus bullockii

SUMMER

Size: 8" (20 cm)

Female: Dull yellow head and chest. Gray-to-black wings with white wing bars. A pale white belly. Gray back, as seen in flight.

Male: bright orange and black bird with a bold white patch on wings

Juvenile: similar to female

Nest: pendulous; female and male build; 1 brood per year

Eggs: 4-6; pale white to gray, brown markings

Incubation: 12-14 days; female incubates

Fledging: 12-14 days; female and male feed young

Migration: complete, to Central and South America

Food: insects, berries, nectar; visits nectar feeders

Compare: Has a grayer back than the female Baltimore (pg. 391). Female Scott's Oriole (pg. 401) is larger and lacks the pale white belly. Female Hooded Oriole (pg. 397) is the same size, but lacks a pale white belly. Look for female Bullock's dull yellow and gray appearance.

Stan's Notes: So closely related to Baltimore Orioles of the eastern U.S., at one time both were considered a single species. Interbreeds with Baltimores where their ranges overlap. Most common in the state where cottonwood trees grow along rivers and other wetlands. Also found at edges of clearings, in city parks, on farms and along irrigation ditches. Hanging sock-like nest is constructed of plant fibers such as inner bark of junipers and willows. Will incorporate yarn and thread into its nest if offered at the time of nest building.

female

male pg. 341

Hooded Oriole
Icterus cucullatus

SUMMER

Size: 8" (20 cm)

Female: A dull yellow head, breast, belly, rump and tail. Gray back and wings with single white wing bars. Black eyes.

Male: orange yellow with black throat, dark wings

Juvenile: similar to adult of the same sex

Nest: pendulous; female and male construct; 1-2 broods per year

Eggs: 3-5; dull white with brown markings

Incubation: 12-14 days; female incubates

Fledging: 12-14 days; female and male feed young

Migration: complete, to Central and South America

Food: insects, fruit, nectar

Compare: Female Bullock's Oriole (pg. 395) is very similar, but has a pale white belly. Female Scott's Oriole (pg. 401) is larger with black on the throat and upper breast.

Stan's Notes: A bird of tree-lined creeks and streams, palm groves, mesquite and arid scrub, often near suburbs. Male courts female with bows while hopping around her, singing a soft song. Points his bill skyward (like many birds in the blackbird family). Female will respond with a similar dance. Constructs an unusual sock-like nest, hung from a twig or woven through a palm leaf. Entrance often near the top, but can be on the side. Takes 3-7 days to build nest of wiry green grass, shredded palm leaves or yucca fibers. Some repair and reuse nests. Sips flower nectar, but not like hummingbirds. Often slices into the base of a flower, bypassing its natural entrance. Young are fed a regurgitate of insects and nectar the first 5-7 days of life.

male pg. 349

female

SUMMER

Summer Tanager
Piranga rubra

Size: 8" (20 cm)

Female: Some show a faint wash of red, but most females are a mustard yellow overall with slightly darker wings.

Male: bright rosy red bird with darker red wings

Juvenile: male has patches of red and green over the entire body, female is same as adult female

Nest: cup; female builds; 1-2 broods per year

Eggs: 3-5; pale blue with dark markings

Incubation: 10-12 days; female incubates

Fledging: unknown days; female and male feed young

Migration: complete, to Central and South America

Food: insects, fruit

Compare: Similar to female Orchard Oriole (pg. 393) and Baltimore Oriole (pg. 391), but female Summer Tanager lacks wing bars and has a larger, thicker bill.

Stan's Notes: Found in Texas where woodlands exist, especially in mixed pine and oak forests. Due to land clearing for agriculture, populations have decreased over the past century and especially during the last two decades. Returning to Texas in late April and with young hatching in late May, some pairs have two broods per year. While fruit makes up some of the diet, most of it consists of insects such as bees and wasps. Summer Tanagers unfortunately seem to be parasitized by Brown-headed Cowbirds.

male

female

Scott's Oriole
Icterus parisorum

SUMMER

Size: 9" (22.5 cm)

Male: A black head, neck, back, upper breast and tail with lemon yellow belly, shoulders and rump. Long, pointed, slightly down-curved black bill. Dark eyes. Two white wing bars.

Female: similar to male, but has much less black

Juvenile: grayer than female, yellow under belly only

Nest: pendulous; female builds; 1-2 broods a year

Eggs: 2-4; pale blue with brown markings

Incubation: 14-16 days; female and male incubate

Fledging: 14-16 days; female and male feed young

Migration: complete, to Mexico

Food: insects, fruit, nectar; will come to orange or grapefruit halves and nectar feeders

Compare: The female Bullock's Oriole (pg. 395) has a pale white belly. Male American Goldfinch (pg. 379) is much smaller and has black on the forehead, not on the entire head.

Stan's Notes: Found in open dry areas often associated with yucca and palm. Like other oriole species, female constructs a sock-like pouch that hangs from the end of a thin branch or is woven into a hole in a palm leaf. Populations have increased over the past 100 years due to planting of palm trees. Male is yellow, not orange, like other male orioles. Hunts by gleaning insects and caterpillars from leaves. Uses its long pointed bill to poke holes in bases of flowers to get nectar. Parents feed their young by regurgitating a mixture of insects and fruit. Named after General Winfield Scott, who fought in the Mexican War.

Western Kingbird
Tyrannus verticalis

SUMMER

Size: 9" (22.5 cm)

Male: Bright yellow belly and yellow under wings. Gray head and chest, often with white chin. Wings and tail are dark gray to nearly black with white outer edges on tail.

Female: same as male

Juvenile: similar to adult, less yellow and more gray

Nest: cup; female and male construct; 1 brood per year

Eggs: 3-4; white with brown markings

Incubation: 18-20 days; female incubates

Fledging: 16-18 days; female and male feed young

Migration: complete, to Central America

Food: insects, berries

Compare: The Eastern Kingbird (pg. 275) lacks any yellow of the Western Kingbird. The Great Kiskadee (pg. 407) shares the yellow belly, but has a black and white head pattern. Western Meadowlark (pg. 405) also shares the yellow belly of Western Kingbird, but has a distinctive black V-shaped necklace.

Stan's Notes: A bird of open country, frequently seen sitting on top of the same shrub or fence post. Hunts by watching for crickets, bees, grasshoppers and other insects and flying out to catch them, then returns to perch. Parents teach young how to hunt, bringing wounded insects back to the nest for the young to chase. Returns in March. Builds nest in April, often in a fork of a small single trunk tree. Nests in trees around farms and homesteads.

Western Meadowlark
Sturnella neglecta

Size: 9" (22.5 cm)

Male: Heavy-bodied bird with a short tail. Yellow chest, brown back and prominent black V-shaped necklace. White outer tail feathers.

Female: same as male

Juvenile: same as adult

Nest: cup, on the ground in dense cover; female builds; 1-2 broods per year

Eggs: 3-5; white with brown markings

Incubation: 13-15 days; female incubates

Fledging: 11-13 days; female and male feed young

Migration: non-migrator to partial migrator

Food: insects, seeds

Compare: Western Kingbird (pg. 403) lacks a black V-shaped necklace. Horned Lark (pg. 145) lacks a yellow breast and belly. Look for a distinct black V on Meadowlark's breast.

Stan's Notes: A bird of open grassy country. Named "Meadowlark" because it's a bird of meadows and sings like the larks of Europe. Best known for its wonderful song–a flute-like, clear whistle. Often seen perching on fence posts, it will quickly dive into tall grass if approached. Conspicuous white markings on each side of its tail, most often seen when flying away. Nest is sometimes domed with dried grass. Not a member of the lark family, it actually belongs to the blackbird family and is related to grackles and orioles. Ranges of Eastern and Western Meadowlarks overlap in the state (map reflects the combined range). The birds are hard to distinguish, but Western is paler yellow and grayer than Eastern and sings a different song.

Great Kiskadee
Pitangus sulphuratus

YEAR-ROUND

Size: 10" (25 cm)

Male: A handsome flycatcher. Bright sulfur yellow chest and belly with a bold black and white striped head. White chin and throat. Dull reddish brown back, wings and tail. Yellow crown patch is concealed.

Female: same as male

Juvenile: similar to adult, but not as brightly colored

Nest: modified cup, ball-shaped, covered; female and male build; 1-2 broods per year

Eggs: 3-6; pale white to cream with brown marks

Incubation: 13-15 days; female incubates

Fledging: 15-20 days; female and male feed young

Migration: non-migrator; moves around to find food

Food: insects, berries, small fish

Compare: Larger than Western Kingbird (pg. 403), which shares a yellow belly but lacks the bold black and white head pattern.

Stan's Notes: Brightly colored flycatcher, unlike most others. Seen in densely vegetated areas and brushy woods near water. Sits in the open, sunning itself and drying out after diving in water for aquatic insects and small fish, which is uncommon in flycatchers. Waits on a perch, watching for passing insects, then flies out to snatch one and returns to the same perch. Often beats prey against a branch several times to stun or kill it before eating. Will usually chase away other birds that enter its territory. Named for its loud, screaming "kiss-ka-dee" call. Also gives a loud "sree-ah." Range is restricted to southern Texas in the U.S., but extends into Central America.

HELPFUL RESOURCES

Birder's Bug Book, The. Waldbauer, Gilbert. Cambridge: Harvard University Press, 1998.

Birder's Dictionary. Cox, Randall T. Helena, MT: Falcon Press Publishing, 1996.

Birder's Handbook, The. Ehrlich, Paul R., David S. Dobkin and Darryl Wheye. New York: Simon and Schuster, 1988.

Birds Do It, Too: The Amazing Sex Life of Birds. Harrison, Kit and George H. Harrison. Minocqua, WI: Willow Creek Press, 1997.

Birds of Forest, Yard, and Thicket. Eastman, John. Mechanicsburg, PA: Stackpole Books, 1997.

Birds of North America. Kaufman, Kenn. New York: Houghton Mifflin, 2000.

Blackbirds of the Americas. Orians, Gordon H. Seattle: University of Washington Press, 1985.

Cry of the Sandhill Crane, The. Grooms, Steve. Minocqua, WI: NorthWord Press, 1992.

Dictionary of American Bird Names, The. Choate, Ernest A. Boston: Harvard Common Press, 1985.

Everything You Never Learned About Birds. Rupp, Rebecca. Pownal, VT: Storey Publishing, 1997.

Field Guide to the Birds, A: A Completely New Guide to All the Birds of Eastern and Central North America. Peterson, Roger Tory and Virginia Marie Peterson. Boston: Houghton Mifflin, 1998.

Field Guide to the Birds of North America: Third Edition. Washington, DC: National Geographic Society, 1999.

Field Guide to Warblers of North America, A. Dunn, Jon and Kimball Garrett. Boston: Houghton Mifflin, 1997.

Field Guide to Western Birds, A. Peterson, Roger Tory. Boston: Houghton Mifflin, 1998.

Folklore of Birds. Martin, Laura C. Old Saybrook, CT: Globe Pequot Press, 1996.

Guide to Bird Behavior, A: Vol I, II, III. Stokes, Donald and Lillian Stokes. Boston: Little, Brown and Company, 1989.

How Birds Migrate. Kerlinger, Paul. Mechanicsburg, PA: Stackpole Books, 1995.

Lives of Birds, The: Birds of the World and Their Behavior. Short, Lester L. Collingdale, PA: DIANE Publishing, 2000.

Lives of North American Birds. Kaufman, Kenn. Boston: Houghton Mifflin, 1996.

Living on the Wind. Weidensaul, Scott. New York: North Point Press, 2000.

National Audubon Society: North American Birdfeeder Handbook. Burton, Robert. New York: Dorling Kindersley Publishing, 1995.

National Audubon Society: The Sibley Guide to Bird Life and Behavior. Edited by David Allen Sibley, Chris Elphick and John B. Dunning, Jr. New York: Alfred A. Knopf, 2001.

National Audubon Society: The Sibley Guide to Birds. Sibley, David Allen. New York: Alfred A. Knopf, 2000.

Photographic Guide to North American Raptors, A. Wheeler, Brian K. and William S. Clark. New York: Academic Press, 1999.

Raptors of Eastern North America: The Wheeler Guides. Wheeler, Brian K. Princeton, NJ: Princeton University Press, 2003.

Raptors of Western North America: The Wheeler Guides. Wheeler, Brian K. Princeton, NJ: Princeton University Press, 2003.

Secret Lives of Birds, The. Gingras, Pierre. Toronto: Key Porter Books, 1997.

Secrets of the Nest. Dunning, Joan. Boston: Houghton Mifflin, 1994.

Sparrows and Buntings: A Guide to the Sparrows and Buntings of North America and the World. Byers, Clive, Jon Curson and Urban Olsson. New York: Houghton Mifflin, 1995.

Stokes Bluebird Book: The Complete Guide to Attracting Bluebirds. Stokes, Donald and Lillian Stokes. Boston: Little, Brown and Company, 1991.

Stokes Field Guide to Birds: Western Region. Stokes, Donald and Lillian Stokes. Boston: Little, Brown and Company, 1996.

Texas Birding Hotlines

To report unusual bird sightings or possibly hear recordings of where birds have been seen, you can often call pre-recorded hotlines detailing such information. Since these hotlines are usually staffed by volunteers, and phone numbers and even the organizations that host them often change, the phone numbers are not listed here. To obtain the numbers, go to your favorite internet search engine, type in something like "rare bird alert hotline Texas" and follow the links provided.

Web Pages

The Internet is a valuable place to learn more about birds. You may find birding on the Net a fun way to discover additional information or to spend a long winter night. These web sites will assist you in your pursuit of birds. If a web address doesn't work (they often change a bit), just enter the name of the group into a search engine to track down the new web address.

Site	Address
Audubon Texas	www.audubon.org/chapter/tx/tx
Audubon in the State of Texas	www.audubon.org/states/tx
American Birding Association	www.americanbirding.org
Cornell Lab of Ornithology	www.birds.cornell.edu
Author Stan Tekiela's home page	www.naturesmart.com

CHECK LIST/INDEX BY SPECIES

Use the boxes to check the birds you've seen.

ABOUT THE AUTHOR

Stan Tekiela is a naturalist, author and wildlife photographer with a Bachelor of Science degree in Natural History from the University of Minnesota. He has been a professional naturalist for more than 20 years and is a member of the Minnesota Naturalist Association, Minnesota Ornithologist Union, Outdoor Writers Association of America, North American Nature Photography Association and Canon Professional Services. Stan actively studies and photographs birds throughout the United States. He has received various national and regional awards for outdoor education and writing. A columnist and radio personality, his syndicated column appears in over 20 cities and he can be heard on a number of radio stations. Stan lives in Victoria, Minnesota, with wife Katherine and daughter Abigail. He can be contacted via his web page at www.naturesmart.com.

Stan authors field guides for other states including guides for birds, birds of prey, mammals, reptiles and amphibians, trees and wildflowers.